Lunch at Toad River

Lunch at Toad River

Moving to Alaska

SALLY LESH

Point Adolphus Press
Gustavus, Alaska USA

◣ **Point Adolphus** Press

PO Box 126
Gustavus, AK 99826
USA

e-mail: info@PointAdolphus.com
web: www.PointAdolphus.com

Lunch at Toad River

First Edition

Library of Congress Control Number: 2001097569

ISBN: 0-9708769-0-4

Printed in Canada

For Jack

Traveling in the company of those we love is home in motion.

— Leigh Hunt
The Indicator, 1821

Map drawn by Carolyn Lesh

Acknowledgments

Thanks to Carol Dejka who turned my hen scratches into legible script. Tom McCabe at Point Adolphus Press who burned many a gallon of midnight oil as he computerized not only the manuscript but also the photographs into a book. Carolyn Lesh who drew the map and our route across it, as well as helped with the cover. The writers' group of Gustavus who encouraged me and helped with commas and capitals. Kitty Baker for her help getting permission to use material from the Cape Cod Times. And David Bohn, Hayden Kaden, Carol McCabe and Margaret Thomas for their copyediting and valuable editorial suggestions.

Sally Lesh

Preface

I'm Sally, sometimes called Sal. My husband Jack and I were living in Falmouth on Massachusetts' Cape Cod with our eight children when we decided to move to Alaska in the late '50s. We had a lovely six-bedroom home on Ransom Road, where we kept a small orchard and raised chickens, goats, turkeys and a huge garden. The beach was a twenty-minute walk or a half-hour rowboat ride away. The schools were fine and Jack's medical practice was flourishing. So why did we leave?

It beats me. I think we wanted more wilderness, having experienced some of it while stationed in Spokane, Washington, during the Korean War.

Jack had graduated from Columbia University Medical School in New York on the GI Bill of Rights. Those years had been hard. The kids kept arriving. We lived in various odd situations but mainly at Camp Shanks in New York. Jack held down a night job at the hospital in New York City and went to school. He sometimes came home on weekends, often to find a sign on the back door — "Quarantine" — chicken pox, mumps, measles and so on. Camp Shanks, a former Army camp, had an enormous population of GIs juggling school and family just like Jack. When he graduated from Columbia, he had more kids and less money than anyone else in his class. Still, he finished among the top ten.

It was fun really. We were young and poor and eager to get on with our lives, which had been violently disrupted by war. After completing his university studies, Jack went to Lansing, Michigan, for his internship. After that, he owed the Air Force two years of service as a doctor, which we spent at Fairchild Air Force Base in Spokane.

We loved the wild country there, miles and miles of forests, rivers and mountains, with the added benefit of perfect weather year round. When those two years were up, we had five boys and Jack needed a job. We looked around that beautiful country but finally he accepted a job in Falmouth, Massachusetts. In 1952 we drove across the country to Falmouth, where, for the next eight years, Jack practiced medicine and I had three more babies.

We had planned on sixteen children but I developed cancer and had a radical mastectomy in 1958. When I returned home from the hospital, I had eight children, a farm and a garden to take care of while my body healed. But young people can do anything and we were relatively young; I was thirty-eight and Jack was thirty-seven.

At the time, more and more people were pouring onto the Cape, chiefly in summer. The locals were becoming more sophisticated and children of twelve were wearing tuxedos and strapless gowns to school dances. So, we decided to pull up stakes and go back to the great sweeps of wild country in the Northwest — or Alaska.

*   *   *   *   *

We have been in Alaska now for more than forty years. A few years ago someone here in our small community started a writers' group. Having nothing better to do that winter than make two quilts, move our community library into a new building and continue working in the old library almost daily, I thought I would try to compile all my notes and the journal from our trip across Canada in 1960.

I do not call myself a writer, I'm not even very good at letters, but the writer's group was very supportive — that latest buzz-word for helpful — and urged me to continue, even going so far as to laugh in the right places.

That's the why of it. This then is the story of our move to Alaska in 1960. At the time, the children's ages were: Michael, 17; Peter, 14; Jonathan, 12; James, 10; David, 9; Sally Ann, 5; Betsy, 4; and Thomas, 2.

This account was written in a daily journal as we planned and executed the trip from start to finish. We enjoyed it, mostly, and I hope you will, too.

Lunch at Toad River

Falmouth, Massachusetts

Actually, we had planned to go to France.

We had wonderful plans for putting the children into some marvelous little school somewhere. While Jack worked at something nebulous but lucrative, I planned to sit around in ravishing cocktail dresses, sipping aperitifs and murmuring devastatingly clever French phrases. I understand French if the few words I know are spoken slowly and distinctly and are accompanied by gestures. But Jack, feeling that this was not enough, enrolled in a night school course called "An Introduction to French," where he learned lots of useful phrases for travelers. One of these was: "Is this your little boy?" I urged him always to answer "No," whether it was our little boy or not. Whomever the boy belongs to, you can bet he just did something dreadful. Another striking example of these useful phrases was the one that went: "Are there carrots or lentils in the soup?" Well, sometimes it's important to know these things. At the end of the year of French lessons, we gave a dinner for the class. The idea was to speak French all evening.

As the guests arrived, Jack met them at the door with, "Comment allez vous ce soir?" To which each and every guest replied brightly, "Je vais tres bien merci, et vous?" Dead silence and deader smiles ensued as people shuffled around taking off boots and coats, blowing noses, while trying to think of something to say in French. So much for all those conversation classes. It looked like a long evening. I passed the sherry. That helped a little but it was just not much fun listening to the French girl, who cooked our dinner, and the teacher chattering away en francais to each other at a rapid-fire pace. Some of the smarter students pretended to understand what was being said and smiled brightly now and then but, really, nobody understood one word. And it was not until we got into the martinis and started speaking American that anyone had any fun at all. I lighted the candles in the dining room and we sat down around the table. The conversation by now was bilingual with American being the lingua franca.

Dinner was as French as could be managed with American ingredients. We dismissed the cheese cart out of hand: Velveeta? American? Our first course was steaming, clear consommé, with a sliver of lemon peel floating on top. I was even able to produce consommé cups, thanks to a lavish wedding gift from my grandmother. Next came a leg of lamb with slivers of garlic embedded in the surface. This was accompanied by small, whole potatoes, which had been roasted in goose fat from a neighboring poultry farmer. We tried for petit pois but could only find Green Giant, a sorry substitute, which was partially saved by the addition of a sprig of mint — well, actually a sprig of dried mint. And a pretty salad of iceberg lettuce was followed by a truly sublime dessert, Poires Helene, poached pears on ice cream with a trickle of chocolate sauce.

Demitasses finished the feast. Tongues and belts were loosened. As the guests left, they suddenly recalled the French class, and made their adieux en francaise. When the party was over, we just knew we were meant for Paris and Paris was meant for us.

I really don't know when this dream slipped away but I think it happened when I had my operation. Jack sat by my bedside, reading. It was mere chance that he decided to read Thoreau's "Walden" at this time; after all, both he and the book had been residing in the same house for years. I guess during those years he was too much occupied with making a living for his rapidly increasing family. He read it as he held my hand or gave me pills and he read the best parts aloud. The words came through the fog of drugs thickly. I barely understood him, but I did get the feeling he was being overly influenced by this book. I was right. He was not only impressed, he was sold.

*   *   *   *   *

"Look," Jack said one day during the winter of 1958, when the pain had subsided and I was feeling more like myself, "this is a dumb way to live. All we're doing is running in circles and never quite catching both ends. Let's stop all this nonsense and find ourselves a hunk of wilderness. The heck with France, we can go there anytime."

Now, the only wilderness I knew anything about besides all that gorgeous country around Spokane, where we had bravely made one or two little camping forays, was up in Vermont and Maine and I thought it was beautiful. There were all those glamorous ski resorts where I could sit around wearing cute ski clothes while modestly admitting that, yes, it was my son who had just won the downhill slalom; or, yes, that beautiful blonde was my daughter. And just last year we had fallen in love with a perfectly charming, if a bit run down, old farmhouse that we could fix up and... but Jack was still talking.

"And while we are at this wilderness finding, let's get the best," he was saying, "and go to Alaska."

Dead silence on my part greeted this suggestion. As he continued to glow and expound on the whole matter, touching briefly on log cabins, root cellars, moose, bears and cozy evenings reading by the woodstove, I realized I would have to change my tactics. Silent glaring wasn't working. So, I shouted.

"NO! ABSOLUTELY NOT! I LOATHE WINTER; I LOATHE being cold and I simply loathe moose. Meese? What-EVER they are. Alaska is a horrid, cold, snowy place and nobody goes there. At least nobody I know goes there."

He had more luck with the boys.

"Mummy and I," he said, graciously including me, "think it might be fun to go and live in the woods somewhere; build a log cabin; go fishing and hunting for our food; learn to live off the land away from civilization; and well, how would you like that?"

"Oh boy! No school you mean, Dad?" asked Jon.

"Gosh! No bathtubs either. Gee, Dad!" from Peter.

"Why don't we go to Alaska, Dad?" said Jim. "We're studying about Alaska in school now and the book says they have summer and flowers and everything."

It was as easy as that. My vote didn't even count because no-body heard it in the din.

*   *   *   *   *

From then on the whole family did nothing but talk about Alaska, read about Alaska and ask about Alaska. Jack brought home as many books as he could find from the local library that had anything to say about Alaska. And when we had read those he sent to the Boston libraries for more. It all sounded very exciting, I must say. But it also sounded very cold. And dark. And desolate. Boy, did it sound desolate! The books had interesting little stories about wolves stalking hunters, or bears wrecking cab-ins, or snow that was seven feet deep and lasted all winter. Then there were the stories of trappers caught in their own traps and freezing to death. And the terrible thing was, these stories were true. People in log cabins were always running out of food in the dead of winter or running high fevers miles and miles from the nearest town. I really wasn't much taken by what I had been read-ing, especially when I noticed a strange similarity to all the stories. These adventurous, intrepid couples who dared the long, dark winters and lived to write about them, had no children! I guess that's how they found the time to write.

The books also had lots of pictures, mostly amateur photo-graphs of dowdy women with dreadful hairdos who wore, to a woman, great bulky mackinaw jackets and heavy boots. They looked too dreary for words and I had no desire to join their ranks. Not that I am any clotheshorse. I really look pretty dread-ful most of the time. For fifteen years, children and babies have been bleeding or spitting up on me and, no matter what I do, I cannot get rid of the smell of bleach. But I know how I'm supposed to look and every now and then, when society demands my presence, I do make a gigantic effort to look like a real person. If I start out good and early in the morning by trying to find a pair of nylons that either match or have no runs, and spend the entire day doing things to my hair and nails and pores, I can, by evening, look quite nice. Especially if I am in a non-pregnant phase. While I wasn't really eager to look like those hearty women in gumboots, the wilderness did sound appealing: clean white snow and the peace and quiet. As long as it wasn't too far to town, I figured things could be worse.

No plumbing, for example. That's the worst thing I can think of happening to anybody. Camping out is okay because you can go back home in a week or two, taking the dirty clothes and dishes with you. Then, while the dishes are in the dishwasher and the clothes are swishing around in a shiny, white washing machine, you can swish around in a lovely hot scented bath. But to go on day after day, week in and week out, washing all the dishes, pots, kettles, children and overalls in one small pan, with water that must be heated on a woodstove, which in turn must be fed with logs constantly, well, that is a horse of a different color, believe me. Suppose you were faced with ten pairs of filthy overalls, a small tub, a kettle of hot water and a bar of soap! What then? And, of course, in interior Alaska where it gets really cold, forty below, for instance, all the plumbing freezes solid and you have to melt snow and ice for all those little chores. What do you do then if you have three children who are throwing up and having diarrhea?

The whole scene was too dismal and dispiriting to contemplate, so I pushed those thoughts far from my mind, assuming that, when the time came, I could make some sort of arrangement. Maybe some woman with fewer children might take the blue jeans and pound them in a stream for me. I went on to read more about the beauty of the North. And it sounded grand, all that quiet.

"But what about the children's schooling?" I asked, grasping at any straw.

"Oh that," Jack said decisively. "I've already written both the U. S. Bureau of Education and the Canadian one, in case we decide to settle in Canada. There are good correspondence courses for kindergarten through high school and all we have to do is supervise the children while they do their lessons. Lots of families do it that way."

I had this mental picture of me in a log cabin with all eight children. They were bent diligently over their books while I stirred something on the woodstove. The only sound was Jack's axe as he cut down a tree. The picture grew until it assumed movie-like proportions. The sheep would be grazing on a nearby mountain meadow. I would be serenely standing at the stove wearing a dress of homespun, the wool for which Jack and the boys would have sheared and I would have washed and dyed, carded and spun, woven and sewed. The two little girls would be sitting quietly on their bunks, cleverly knitting mittens. Hand-knitted socks would be drying over the stove. Bread would be baking, while three sweet-smelling pies cooled on the windowsill.

But this movie scene was as unreal as it was enchanting. I knew home schooling would be another matter entirely. As I considered the advantages and disadvantages of such an education, I finally came down on the side of formal schooling, by real teachers, not frantic mothers with questionable talents. For example, I simply cannot understand numbers. Problems in simple addition or subtraction baffle me. If the children ever ask me to help them with their long division, I go to pieces. I would be no help at all with mathematics. History is so dull I can't bear to think about it. There are all those many dates to remember and names and battles. I can only imagine that history would be passed over lightly.

Reading and writing are my best subjects but, in the wilderness, where in the world would all the books come from? At home, if I bring home ten or twelve books from the library, the boys read them in a week. That's an awful lot of books to carry in a backpack over a long trail, along with the groceries.

I could not get too excited about all this education at home but Jack wasn't the least bit daunted. He just brought home more books. There were books on wildlife and books on hunting and trapping; there were books on building log cabins and blazing trails; and there was one treasure that told us how to live off the land.

Apparently, there is no need to starve to death if you happen to be in the wilderness with no food and no gun. Why, food abounds on every hand and all you have to do is know where to find it and how to get it.

"Just scratch down under the snow and you'll find tender little lemmings hibernating in their burrows," says the book. If you happen to be in the part of the country where lemmings live, you're all set. Frankly, I don't know if I would recognize a lemming if I met one but I do know that it would be most difficult to grab one of those cute little sleepy animals and eat it. What a disgusting thought, to have the thing go down fighting.

"Look over your head," says the book. "Reach up and pull the tender tips off the spruce branches. These make a nourishing tea." If you have a fire and a pot to boil water in. But supposing you are like me and call every tree that has needles a pine tree? How in the world would you know a spruce from a hemlock?

"In certain parts of the Northwest the Eskimos and Indians use rabbit droppings as thickening in their soups and stews," the book goes on to explain. All I can say is, I hope I never meet any of these folks; they might invite me to share a stew and I might be unladylike about it.

Then comes the best part of all: "Be sure to eat all parts of all animals. In this way you are assured that you will receive the necessary vitamins and minerals." And the author goes on to write glowingly about Roast Moose Nose and Fried Beaver Tail. But here's the part that really electrified me: "The contents of a moose stomach are not unlike a tossed salad."

"Now see!" said Jack happily. "I shoot a moose and we'll have a salad." This chapter did it for me. I just didn't read any more books on survival and stuck to the more conventional stories of starvation and death by freezing.

Somehow though, somewhere during that winter of reading, I was gradually won over. I was beginning to think in terms of "when we go" rather than "if we go." What finally tipped the balance was the series of episodes with the Cub Scouts.

*   *   *   *   *

I really don't know why I ever fell for the Cub Scout program, but I did. It must be the dumbest program ever thought up for the edification or education of the young American male. Every young boy I knew was just dandy at taking care of himself. I don't think our boys ever said, "What can we do now?" They all tried it once or twice when they were younger, but I fixed them in a hurry by telling them they could clean the chicken house or take care of the babies for a couple of hours. From then on, it was never a problem. They knew what they were going to do the minute school let out in the afternoon; all that they required was a peanut butter sandwich and a glass of milk to keep body and soul together until dinner.

Our little Cub Scout den started out with five boys, three of them mine, the other two close neighbors and pals. At first we followed the party line, learned the rules and pledges and played along with the games and activities, which began to pall before too many meetings had passed. There seemed to be more interest in the cookies than the program, but we persevered and all went well for a couple of months. One day, I received an invitation in the mail.

```
Dear Den Mother,

We would like to help you get the most out of
Cubbing. We have a bang-up program full of new
ideas for your Den Meetings:  activities, songs,
games and much more. We do want you to be there.
Don't let us down. Your Den Dad will be there, too,
learning with you.

The meeting will be held on Tuesday at 7 PM at the
Woods Hole Fire Hall.  Refreshments will be served.

Sincerely in Scouting,
Your Pack Leader
```

It was the first time I had heard of a Den Dad. I knew how Jack would react if he knew I had a Den Dad to learn about Cubbing with, so I just didn't mention it at home. Well, I went to the meeting, and there I met my Den Dad. He wasn't a bit cute; he was fat, phlegmatic and smelled of cigars. I put on a brave front and ignored him.

After we demonstrated that we knew the Cub Scout Pledge, we were shown a movie, which had neither point nor plot but was full of pithy remarks such as, "Come on Mom! Join the fun!" and "Let's keep our youngsters happily learning." At this point in the program, the scoutmaster in charge became quite kittenish and proposed a game. We, all of us, grown men and women, arranged ourselves in a circle and, as we sort of sidestepped around in a crab-like manner, we were supposed to flap our arms and say "choo-choo-choo." The point of that game escaped me, too.

After this we had one more meeting, the Cubs and I, which was so successful that I pass it on to you Den Mothers who are desperate. We made a kite, climbed a hill to a large, open field and, with much effort, managed to get the thing aloft. When it was way, way up in the sky and nobody was looking, I let go of the string. Shrieking dramatically, "Get that kite, boys," I fled home to the kitchen. They all disappeared over the hill in earnest pursuit.

It wasn't until almost suppertime that they all came back, defeated. In the meantime, I had had a cup of hot tea laced with brandy, and written a letter of resignation to my Den Dad. I think the boys were as relieved as I was. Once again they were free to do what they pleased after school.

"If we have to do things with our children," said Jack, "let's at least do something fun like building a log cabin to live in, or hunting for our food. Can't we get them away from ice cream stands and movies? Can't we escape from the P.T.A. and women's clubs and children's clubs? These appear to add only nuisance value to both their lives and ours. Let's go," he finished, "and the sooner the better."

*   *   *   *   *

Now the planning started in earnest.

It was kind of fun deciding what things were really essential and what things we could get along without. A mixer? I have perfectly good muscles and can whip up a batch of bread or cookies without much trouble and, when you come right down to it, it is easier to wash one spoon and a pair of hands than all the gadgets for the mixer. So, no mixer. Blender? I've only had one since last Christmas and have used it twice; I guess we don't need that. Obviously pots and pans and dishes would be needed and, since our family is large, the pots must be also. I started out the essential list with my heavy five-gallon stockpot in order to have a soup going most of the time. That's what they did in the books. Next, my two pressure cookers to tenderize tough wild game, and a hand-turned meat grinder for the same purpose. My huge iron skillet I simply could not get along without; we have been together at every meal for the last ten years and I'd be lost without it. Two medium-sized saucepans and the old iron kettle Jack's grandmother used for rendering fat made up the cooking vessels. I added a large colander with legs; bread and pie tins; a griddle; and two large, shallow baking pans for cakes or biscuits or even roasts.

Each person had to have dishes so the set of heavy, plastic dishes was considered essential, by me at any rate. Jack was content with the surplus Army plates, which were divided into three sections and nested nicely into a small, compact pile. But I felt that there would be times when we would like to have several courses in succession instead of all at once. Our traveling kitchen also included: plastic tumblers; heavy china cups, the kind you find in roadside diners; silverware and mixing utensils; a bean pot and a teapot. I felt that, thus equipped, I could face the wilderness and the woodstove with confidence.

Next came the books. Jack had all sorts of book lists. One listed books to give away. One was labeled, "Not Good Enough to Keep if We Must Carry Them." His favorite list, which he kept adding to, was, "These Go Down with the Ship." This one included: books that the children should read; books he intended to use as supplementary study material; all sorts of how-to books, including that nifty one about living off the land, just in case I should forget how to thicken a soup; books on stars, navigation, weather and survival; books of poetry, plays and first-aid — well, just about anything you could think of.

Next came tools with which to build a log cabin and perform other chores. The usual carpenter's tools went in, but at least three of everything, so that three people could be building the cabin while the others were engaged in other pursuits, such as hunting, fishing or cooking. The tool collection also included two pipe saws and a two-man saw, a sledgehammer, shovels, a rake, crowbars, wedges, axes — we had seven of these — and a vise. Then there were boxes and boxes of strange and wonderful objects like hasps, bolts and wires, which I assumed were needed in house building.

We planned kits for every imaginable possibility and Jack made lists of things to go in the kits. There was a Leather-Fixing Kit full of bits of leather and tools to fix shoes or harnesses or belts. There was a Letter-Writing Kit with all the necessary items in it, even refills for the ballpoint pens, paperclips and stamps. There was my Sewing Kit, which I managed to put together without one of his lists. Of course, I forgot the most important item: buttons.

There was a Quiet-Games Kit containing cards, puzzles, tricks and word games. There was a First-Aid Kit, which was a marvel of planning. Jack got quite carried away with his boxes and kept filling wee boxes to fit inside larger boxes, which fit into yet larger ones. Then he made Survival Kits that each person was supposed to wear every time he left camp. These contained a compass, a knife, some fishhooks and line, fine copper wire, Band-Aids, aspirin, waterproof matches in a waterproof case, a piece of rubber tubing (for slingshot, tourniquet, etc.), a signaling mirror with directions for its use printed on the underside, and extra glasses for those who wore them. These were packed neatly into canvas covers, which Jack made to be worn on the belt.

Right about then I decided to have one private chest in which I could pack some things I knew the children would like to have, especially if we were far from civilization. In went a box of all the favorite Christmas tree ornaments, some crayons, coloring books, puzzles and the very favorite storybooks for bedtime reading to the young ones. Then in went some yarn so I could knit in the long, cold evenings — enough for several sweaters, mittens and socks — and a large selection of needles. Into the private chest went my watercolors and some pads of paper; a box of ladies' hardware with things like cup hooks, thumbtacks, small nails, extra parts for the pressure cookers, and all sorts of little odds and ends of this and that. You never know. I even put in a tablecloth and some pretty yellow candles in case we ever had a party.

*   *   *   *   *

The next question was: How to travel.

I, of course, was all for a trailer with overnight stops at nice motels with hot water and clean beds. Jack mentioned the possibility of doing the trip in two cars but the ramifications of that were a bit daunting. What if one of us took a wrong turn? What if one of us passed the other who was making a tinkle stop? What if…? We scratched that idea. The boys thought a covered wagon would be quite the thing. But when all the suggestions were pooled — having thrown out the one made by Jim that we simply walk — it was generally agreed that a bus would be the answer. A school bus.

So it was off to Boston for a tour of secondhand car parks. At first we saw nothing but old, scrappy cars, and nothing that would accommodate ten people for who knew how long. Finally, one salesman recalled having seen a school bus in a competitor's lot and gave us the address.

* * * * *

"A bus! Are you nuts, man?"

"To Alaska? My God, are you crazy?"

"Hey, Fred! Here's a guy wants to drive to Alaska in a school bus! And he's got eight kids!" But do you know something? Every one of those used-car dealers got a sort of faraway look in his eye and more than one said to us, "You know, for two cents I'd throw up this job and go there. I've always wondered what it would be like to live up there, but hell, the wife would never leave. You know how it is."

We drove to the address where a bus had been seen. There it stood in all its yellow glory. We inquired about its history from the lot man. It had been used as the bus for a school band. It had a large rack on top, used to transport instruments, and inside there were racks along each side for luggage. It was just perfect. It looked clean and it sounded as though it would run. We paid the man and Jack triumphantly drove off. I followed in the Volkswagen right behind. We resembled a large, unwieldy ship with a dinghy in tow but we didn't care. When we drove into our yard at home, the boys went wild. They took their first ride sitting in the rack on top while Jack drove them out to the highway and back, tooting and waving to all the neighbors.

It wasn't long before Jack and Mike had the seats unbolted and removed. Soon after, the heated discussions about Arrangement of the Interior were held. Some wanted ten seats and ten bunks; some wanted hammocks; and some even thought beds built into the rack on top would be just dandy fun. Some people wanted hot and cold water while others wanted a built-in root-beer cooler. All this discussion, some quite heated and leading to name-calling and fisticuffs on more than one occasion, led to confusion. Jack was forced to make yet another list.

"If we are going to Alaska in a bus," (and by this time it was quite clear that we were), "and if we are going to spend the winter there in a log cabin of our own building, what will we need for this undertaking?" Having already made several lists to this effect, it was soon borne in upon us, as we surveyed the inside of the bus, that we would need two buses. So we made new lists. One was labeled, "Things We Cannot Do Without on the Trip," and the other was labeled, "Things We Cannot Do Without in a Log Cabin in an Alaska Winter." What remained to be done was to find room on the bus for all these needed items and we would be set.

Obviously, there would be no room for every one of us to sleep in the bus at the same time. But I absolutely insisted on one bed anyway for napping children or a tired father. Since there was no room to sleep on the bus, we would have to sleep outside it. Naturally, I brought up the subject of motels again but was shouted down by more adventurous souls, everyone else. We would make a teepee.

Sure, it was a real teepee — as real as I could make it on my little old sewing machine. I was fascinated with teepees at the age of ten when I read Ernest Thompson Seton's book, "Two Little Savages." This marvel of a temporary home is, to my mind, the very best of all tents. You can walk around in it; you can hang things up overhead; and, best of all, you can build a fire in the center and be warm and cozy. The roundness seems to give comfort, too.

As no buffalo lived on Cape Cod for skins, I needed a lot of canvas. From the instructions in the book, I determined that we would need one hundred yards of treated canvas that was twenty-nine inches wide to construct the teepee. There was much excitement when the heavy roll was delivered to our door. I could hardly lift it but the boys and Jack pitched in and we carried it out to the lawn. There we unrolled it and cut the strips according to our carefully worked out lengths. These were numbered at each end and stacked in order, with the longest strips on the bottom of the pile and the shortest ones on top.

Our dining room table was long and narrow, perfect for the job of sewing that lay ahead. With Jack on one side of the old

Singer sewing machine and a boy behind me we slowly fed the first two strips into the machine and stitched the length of it. I ran a second line of stitching for strength. Next came the rest of the strips, one at a time. With each succeeding strip the job became harder as the bulk and heaviness grew. When we got to the long strips at the bottom everyone was helping. One boy was backing up Jack and three more were behind me, holding the heavy stuff so it would feed through the machine properly. Even with all these precautions, I broke several needles and when the last backstitch was finished at the end of the last long seam we all collapsed on the floor amid what seemed to be acres and tons of canvas. Then it was rolled up and set aside, waiting for a spell of sunny weather for painting.

When that day came, we were ready. The bundle was carried to the big field out back, spread on the ground and smoothed. We had decided, after much excited discussion, to paint a wide band of green about a yard high around the bottom to make that lower part more waterproof. Then came a band of black footprints — Black Foot tribe, of course, which in this case was apt. Then a buffalo, complete with embedded arrow and drips of blood, bucking horses and arrows galore. It was quite a sight and would have reduced any Indian of any tribe to helpless laughter. But we thought it was beautiful.

The next thing was poles. Jack and the boys went off to the woods to cut these. The project kept them busy for days after school, stripping the bark and removing all the little knots so the canvas wouldn't be torn as it was dragged across them. I made many buttonholes on the long straight side of the teepee canvas. Theoretically, when the canvas was wrapped around the poles these would overlap and be laced together with small sticks. I also cut and hemmed a smoke flap and stitched it into place.

Then came the great day when we set it up for the first time. The canvas was secured permanently with line near the top of one pole, leaving a long tail. Three more poles were tied together permanently and set on the ground, opened out at the bottom in the shape of a tripod. A long tail of line hung down from the top of these, also. One boy grabbed and hung onto this rope dangling from the tripod to set it securely on the ground. Next, the rest of the poles were leaned on this tripod, spacing them in a circle roughly fourteen feet in diameter. When these were all in place, the pole with the canvas attached to it was laid in place and two people, in this case two boys, each grabbed a side of canvas and walked around the poles until they met at the opposite side, which would be the door. The bag of lacing sticks was found and the two flaps were laced together. The very last pole was poked into the pocket of the smoke flap and propped to one side, awaiting a campfire or rain, when it would be needed. Everything was then tightened up, ground stakes were hammered through loops on the bottom edge and the teepee was ready for occupancy.

It took a little longer to set up than a regular tent. We figured the boys could use a little exercise setting up the teepee at the end of a long day's travel.

On the metal rack on top of the bus we found a place for the poles, while the canvas part was rolled up into a compact bundle and assigned shelf space inside the bus.

Neither Jack nor I thought it would be much fun to sleep with the boys in the teepee. We bought ourselves a small green tent to use as the master bedroom. We would take the baby, as two-year-old Tom was still called, in the tent with us. The two girls would sleep on the bed in the bus. Now, the Problem of Sleeping was solved.

My next thoughts were for the kitchen. An army travels on its stomach and we were a small army.

A folding, wood-burning stove, commonly called a Yukon stove, was what we decided on for cooking because wood would be available everywhere. Then too, there were those five boys with all that energy who, after putting up the teepee, would be happy to gather wood for the supper fire! We added a small gas-burning camp stove for times when all the wood was wet or we just wanted a quick pot of tea or a lunchtime soup on a rainy cold day. Next, I packed the trunks. The green one held all the pots and pans, dishes and silverware needed to prepare and serve a meal. This trunk was a masterpiece of planning. I neither regretted nor longed for a single item on the entire trip, and, as usual, it was Jack and his lists that deserved the credit. Remember too, that these kitchen articles were to make do in a log cabin for the whole first winter, or at least until we had the rest of our things shipped out to us.

Here is what my indispensable list narrowed down to:

1 twelve-inch, cast-iron skillet, two- or three-inches deep
  (the one I can't live without)
1 large saucepan
1 large frying pan
1 small frying pan
1 medium kettle, about three quarts
1 small kettle, about two quarts
Coffee pot
Very large stainless steel mixing bowl
Medium-size stainless steel mixing bowl
2 small stainless steel bowls
1 six-quart pressure cooker
1 square baking pan, for rolls or small cakes
2 layer-cake pans with removable bottoms
2 pie tins
2 bread tins
1 one-quart measure
1 one-cup measure
12 Army surplus compartmented plates, metal
12 plastic soup bowls
Pot holders
Silverware for twelve
Various small utensils for cooking
Sharp knives and a sharpening stone
Five-gallon stock pot with a cover

The other trunk, the red one, was packed with food items which would be needed all the time. For the most part, these ingredients were packed in metal containers and the list looked something like this: flour, sugar, brown sugar, pancake mix, corn meal, oatmeal, jam, syrup, baking powder, baking soda, spices and a few other staples. Jack made the cutest little spice rack that fit right into one end of the trunk next to the knife rack.

The dishwashing department consisted of two square plastic dishpans, two pails for water, a dish mop, metal pot cleaner, dishrag and dishtowels. All of these items fit nicely together and were assigned shelf space. We added an enormous basket we had found at the dump, which was to be used as a grocery bin. I ordered a sixteen-pound pail of peanut butter and filled several boxes with home-canned goods — just in case. A little chutney or homemade relish might be just the thing to perk up that roasted moose nose.

The next problem I had to lick was that of washing and drying clothes. Even in a house with a washer and dryer the job assumes epic proportions. But there might be weeks before we ran into a laundromat, because we wanted, that is Jack wanted, to drive on back roads in order to be in wilderness areas as much as possible. It appeared necessary to devise other means of washing clothes.

A friend of ours, an old hand at trailer living, came up with what seemed to be a novel and sensible way of managing. "You buy," he told us, "a large plastic garbage pail with a lock-on lid. In the morning you toss in your soiled clothes, some hot water and soap and you clamp down the lid. At the end of the day, when you reach your campsite, you just take out the clothes, rinse them in the river and hang them up to dry. The motion of the bus will have acted like a washing machine and the clothes will be clean." What could be simpler? I went right downtown to the hardware store where loud laughter greeted my explanations and there was much head shaking. I added an old-fashioned wringer, which I found in a second-hand store, and a tin scrub board. That completed the laundry department and I felt as though I had coped with that problem.

Clothes? Old dungarees for everyone, and plenty of long johns, of which I had bought out the entire supply at the local thrift shop. The ladies there were delighted, as they had despaired of ever selling them. I also gathered sweaters, rubber boots, bathing suits, pajamas and so on. I insisted on good clothes for everyone, choosing the bright blue sailor dresses I had made for the girls, a dress for myself and one good shirt each for the boys and Jack.

Then I spent one ghastly hot day up in the attic, filling a large trunk with heavy cold-weather clothes. The trunk was of the old-fashioned steamer type and had often accompanied my grandmother to Europe many years ago. Once she had invited twenty-one friends to go to Switzerland with her and I am sure this very same trunk went on that trip. And now it was being prepared for a trip to Alaska. I was very proud of the organization of that trunk because I am not ordinarily the organized type. I managed to pack two pairs of mittens, both mended and matching, plus a pair of leather ones for each child and Jack. I also packed a hat apiece and two pairs of heavy wool socks, also mended and matching. Some trick, I'll tell you, since every mother knows these mittens had to be found first, then washed and mended, put into a labeled plastic bag that was, in turn, packed with the owner's heavy jacket, snow pants, hat and scarf. I really earned a Good Housekeeping medal that day.

Sleeping comfort came next and was dispatched with Jack's usual forthright thoroughness. Each person would need a down sleeping bag since we would, in all probability, use them in the aforementioned log cabin, as well as along the way. So we purchased Army surplus sleeping bags for the boys, a double down-filled bag for the master bedroom and two small Dacron bags for the girls. I made a warm, cozy thing for Tom to sleep in. Each boy had, as well, a ground cloth and an air mattress. Jack and I had a big air mattress and a heavy ground cloth to go under everything.

Space was assigned on the luggage racks over the seats for each person to stow his own sleeping bag and personal gear. Personal gear consisted of: a cigar box.

Jack liked cigar boxes. In fact, they are probably his most favorite things, except for empty jars and cans. For weeks now he had been asking all the drugstores to save cigar boxes for him. It was my job to collect them. Every time I came home from a trip downtown, he would ask if I had remembered to pick up the cigar boxes. I think clerks at the stores thought I was nuts but I kept telling them the boxes were for my husband. When we had about forty cigar boxes, Jack said I could stop asking for more. Now it was his turn to start collecting small, plastic boxes that would fit inside the others. As he was a doctor at this time, he began to bring home some of the dozens of tiny pill boxes that arrived at his office through the mail.

One night at supper, Jack announced that this would be Box Night. He gave each one of us a lovely empty cigar box, with its wonderful smell, and a small assortment of smaller plastic ones. He gave us a lecture, too: "Now, these boxes are for your own personal junk. If I ever find one lying around loose I'll throw it out the window. Keep it in your cubby and keep your junk in it." He didn't scare any of us though. We knew he could never bring himself to throw away a box.

*   *   *   *   *

After buying the bus during the summer of 1959, we decided to make a few trips, shakedown cruises as it were, to see how things would go. There was a small ski hill north of Boston where one of Jack's medical partners had a cabin. It was perfect for sleeping, eating and drying out.

On one occasion, I took our five boys and some of their friends to this ski area for a weekend. I made an enormous amount of beef stew, six loaves of bread, dozens of hardboiled eggs and a large cake. I brought gallons of milk to go with it. As we would not be getting home until late Sunday night, I also had to prepare the food for a late supper after our return, plus have ingredients on hand for breakfast on Monday morning and school lunches for my six children.

The trip was mostly successful, though Jim's jacket became tangled in the tow rope and he was dragged almost into the wheel before the operator finally saw him and stopped the motor. Then, one of the girls on the trip with us threw up in the middle of the night after the fire had gone out, so there was only ice water to clean up the mess. Another child got diarrhea on the way home. I was tired to death of children, snow and driving, only to have the bus break down about halfway home. We didn't have too far to walk to a phone to call Jack, who along with another parent drove the eighty miles to our rescue. It was on this trip that we discovered our fuel consumption: eight miles to the gallon.

Alaska was how far? Five thousand miles?

On another memorable trip, we almost became history. It was a day trip down the Cape and Jack's brother-in-law was driving. He slowed at a railroad crossing, but I, under the assumption that no trains had run there for years, told him to go on — it was perfectly safe to cross.

It was not. No sooner had we crossed the tracks than a train came roaring down behind us. And I mean just behind us.

*   *   *   *   *

After much talk, it was decided that we would replace enough seats in the bus to enable the ten of us to be seated at one time, plus two extra, in case of hitchhikers. Jack made two tables that were fastened to the wall between two seats, but which could be removed and lowered to make a bed on each side for emergency situations. The arrangement went like this: the front seats on either side were exactly as they had been in the original setup, facing forward. Directly behind, the next two seats were reversed so they faced the rear and the table. Across the table, two more seats faced forward making little booths permitting eight people to sit at a table. Right behind the last seat on the left, as you faced the rear of the bus, Jack and Mike built in a bed. The bed butted up to a solid wall that separated the kitchen equipment from the rest of the bus. Behind the last seat on the right they built in a hefty workbench, complete with vise, theorizing that we would need one when we started to build that log cabin he was always talking about. After stocking its shelves and drawers with tools, Jack was ready to turn his attention to shelves for the duffel bags.

The duffel bags were Jack's brainchild from first to last. "Each person will have his own and should be responsible for it at all times," he stated. He bought an old treadle sewing machine for one dollar, learned to run it and proceeded to sew up ten duffel bags. They were cylindrical, about thirty inches long, and had a zipper the whole length of one side. These zippers had the added feature of a slide at each end so the bag could be opened from either end. Then he sewed webbing handles on one end and on the side next to the zipper, painted names on the end with the handle and that was that. Next, he and Mike built good solid shelves just for the duffel bags and everyone was assigned a space. More shelves were built under these for other things. I had to have space for my private trunk, which I was still packing and unpacking and re-packing daily, and they made a spot for that. Behind the wall, which supported these shelves, he nailed in a small chest of drawers to hold the hundreds of small items we wanted to take along. Above that, he installed a closet rod to hold the jackets on hangers and the airtight plastic clothes bag, which held everyone's "good" clothes.

When all this was done, there were nooks and crannies everywhere, which could be, and were, stuffed with more things. Jack made a nifty big flat box to go under the bed, and in it he packed the guns, wrapped up in his homemade padded-canvas gun cases. This box would have to be somewhat available when we went through customs in Canada. There, the customs agents would have to seal them. While other things were pushed in here and there on the inside of the bus, up on top of the bus the rack was gradually filling up with large bulky items: a woodstove to use in the cabin, two enormous spare tires, the teepee poles, the trunk containing the winter clothes I had spent so much time packing, a canoe for fishing on lakes, and a couple of five-gallon cans for stove gas.

We had set our departure date as May 22. The boys would be out of school by then and Jack would see his last patients the week before. Of course, the boys became more and more excited as the date approached, while I became more and more an automaton. Not only were we filling the bus, we also were trying to rent the house for the summer, giving us the additional chores of emptying all the closets, drawers and shelves. We also had to go on making meals, washing clothes, caring for the three youngest children and going to farewell parties. It was a busy time. Every day the boys came home from school to find a new list of jobs to be done and they had fun crossing off the lists as fast as Jack made them. Jack gave himself lists of things to do while I just raced in circles trying to keep up with it all and ran errands, most of which had to be done "right now."

"Sal, would you have time to get me a half pound of galvanized Phillips screws about an inch long? And while you are in the hardware store, would you also get fifty feet of three-quarter-inch rope and... well, I guess I'd better make a list for you."

"Mummy, I have to bring a bird's nest to school tomorrow, and since you are going downtown anyway, you could just drop me off at Bill's and I could get a neat one from his yard that I know about. And then you could pick me up again on your way home."

"Hey Mum! Will you get a book from the library for me? Here's the name of the book and I think this is the author... maybe its the other way around... well, ask the lady. Okay, then... I'll just come and ask her myself."

"Mummy! Mummy! Wait! I want to come, too. So does Bets. She's coming... I think I hear Tommy crying and that means he wants to come along but I think he has to go to the bathroom first. Wait for me!" And when we're all finally aboard and halfway out the driveway, I remember I have left the list on the dining room table and must go back and get it. This went on day after day and I became more and more confused about the whole thing. When people said, "My dear, I simply don't know how you manage with eight children; it's all I can do to manage just one," to tell the truth, I wondered how I was managing, too.

The Journey

May 21, 1960

Everything is done.

The house is so neat and tidy and clean it is positively spooky. I hate it this way. Sitting here at the long table, which we have sat around three times a day for eight years, I am lost in a whirlwind of memories. Three of the children were brought home here from the hospital where they were born: Sally Ann, Betsy and Tom. This house and the surrounding woods, pond and beach are the only world Jimmy and David have known, as we moved here when they were very young. Maybe Jon and Pete remember some of the other homes we have had, certainly Mike does. But we have loved it here and put down long roots. For me at least, it will be hard to leave, hard to pull up those roots.

I recall summer mornings when the boys worked in the gardens. As they bent over the plants, their backs brown in the hot sun, they called out to one another. Afternoons their shouts would come gaily across the pond as they splashed in and out and under the water, over and under the rowboat; and evenings I could see their campfire reflected across the dark water when they camped out on the point. Winter mornings I watched them leave for school, shouting, running in the cold and frosty air, banging their lunch pails and waving good-bye. And I remember long, lazy winter evenings around the fireplace. I recall thin winter sunshine over the pond as Jack's mother and I sat knitting together during the day's one quiet hour. All the good times with wonderful friends whirl around in my head as I go to shut the front door for the last time. The moonlit pond is still, the children and Jack are asleep and tomorrow we leave. Perhaps we shall never return.

May 22

Today started with a bang and has been completely out of hand ever since. I hope I never see another day like it as long as I live. It all started at 6:00 a.m. with a determined loud knocking at the back door. I pulled on my dungarees and an old shirt of Jack's, which happened to be handy, and went to open the door. There stood a tall string bean of a young man who had no less than three very expensive cameras slung around his neck. He was accompanied by a young pretty girl. She was carrying a notebook and pencil and smilingly explained that they were from Life magazine and that they were to "cover our trip," at least the first day of it. I raced back into the house, changed into a skirt and blouse, combed my hair and took special pains with my lipstick.

Then I made another appearance at the back door, trying to look both glamorous and casual, only to find the photographer snapping pictures of Bets and Tom, who were happily playing in the dirt, and who never noticed him. So I arranged myself dramatically on the back fence and called the children to me. What an enchanting picture it would make, the children clustered around their mother's knee, their eager, shining faces upturned to her. At that instant, we all heard Mildred's bugle.

Weeks earlier, our warm-hearted neighbor, Mildred, had rashly promised to make sausages and pancakes for us on our day of departure. Furthermore, she had promised, also rashly, to serve coffee to all the folks who came to see us off. Here she was with the prearranged signal: the bugle. All the kids ran off to Mildred's leaving me sitting there on the fence feeling and looking rather foolish. The photographer ran after them, snapping off pictures as he went, with the pretty reporter right after him. So I forgot about posing and went back into the house for some last-minute things: the bottle of rye, the potty and the clothes from the dryer. Jack warmed up the bus and we drove it over to Mildred's, folding clothes and tooting all the way.

Jack parked the bus in Mildred's driveway to make it convenient for everyone who had come to see it; we went in to breakfast. Now the reporter, the pretty girl, began asking questions: Why were we going to Alaska? How did we plan to sleep? What route were we going to take? Who was going to do the driving? How old were the children and what were their names? She went on and on. The photographer fellow came awake with the coffee and, for the first time since 6:00 a.m., he stopped taking pictures — just long enough to say to me, "For a person with eight children, I think you have come through it remarkably well."

By this time, the yard was filling up with friends and neighbors who had come to say good-bye and wish us well. Children swarmed all over the top and sides of the bus. They sat in the rack and yelled at their pals on the ground. People poured in through the front door of the bus, sat on the seats, looked around, poked things and "oohed" and "ahhed" at everything, especially at the two gallons of wine and two bottles of whiskey, which loving and

Ted Polumbaum/TimePix

thoughtful friends had donated. As they jumped out the rear door, they were laughing and shaking their heads.

The photographer took pictures of the neighbors and the neighbors took pictures of the photographer. Two Boston news-papers got into the act and, amid all this shouting and laughing and crying, these reporters wanted to know, "Why are you going to Alaska? What route are you going to take? Who will do the driving? How will you sleep?"… And all the rest of it. I got pretty confused as I tried to name all the children and tell their ages. Then, the neighborhood girls started to cry; a dreadful summer faced them with no boys to pester and I noticed Peter and Jon looking rather smug at this demonstration of affection from girls they professed to despise. All the while, the photographer kept having quaint ideas about how we should pose for him. We lined up for him again and again, as if we were about to embark. It was hard for the younger children to understand what was going on, as we all grabbed our duffel bags, climbed through the front door, walked through the bus, jumped out the rear door, came around to the front and did the whole thing over again.

"Betsy," I said patiently for the fourth time, "get your duffel bag and get on the bus. No, ON the bus."

"Get your bag, Tom, and… NO, Tom! Come back here! The man wants to take a picture of all of us in a line with our duffel bags. Well, I know we did it lots of times but he wants us to do it again. Get up off the ground, Tom, and stop crying! If you don't stop crying this minute I'll go off and leave you. One more time, Bets. That's right, Tom, hold it for just a minute. Sally Ann, look at Daddy and, for heaven's sake, look happy. Now, all together, let's get on the bus. No, Dave, not altogether at once exactly. One at a time. Here goes now: one, two, three, GO!"

Ten a.m. was our planned departure time but Bill, the trusty mechanic who had nursed the bus and Jack through the long months of preparation, had not arrived yet. We felt that, after hours and hours of his time, and hundreds and hundreds of our dollars, we could not go without saying good-bye. At one point, he had even given Jack a new battery saying, "Well, gee, I hate to think of you all going off without an extra battery. Can't ever tell, you know." So we waited a few minutes longer until he showed up and then, of course, the photographer wanted pictures of him and Jack leaning over the motor, with the hood up, having a last-minute consultation. Suddenly, time to leave. Amidst the farewell kisses and wisecracks, a little girl came up to me and, thrusting two small bottles into my hand, she said, "Mrs. Lesh, will you throw this bottle with the note in it into the Pacific Ocean? And will you fill this one with water from the Pacific Ocean and bring it back?" Of course I would.

We were all aboard and the motor was running. We were off! Then, just as Jack pulled out of the driveway and stopped before turning left onto the road, the rear door swung open and John, Mildred's husband, threw aboard a water jug and a coil of rope. "Just in case," he shouted, blew me a kiss and slammed the door shut. We had a police escort out of town as far as the Bourne County line and were followed by a long line of cars, wildly honking and waving. Pete and Jim wanted to ride in the police car with their favorite cop, Elmer, who had shepherded them across the road in front of the school for as long as they could re-member. Friends and patients were standing along the sides of the road for a couple of miles to wave us on our way. I wonder how many of them guessed that, in all probability, we would not be coming back. The police cars stopped at the county line, gave us back the two boys, then, flashing all their lights and blowing their sirens and horns, they turned back to Falmouth and duty. The rest of the cars dropped back and we were on our way in our big yellow school bus, on the way to Alaska.

At this point, comparative quiet settled upon us. The photo-grapher stretched out on the bed for a nap. The reporter curled up on a seat and napped, also. We had a goodly sip of grog, even though the sun was far from the yardarm, and Jack headed the bus towards Purgatory Chasm, a state park just south of Worcester, Massachusetts, where various members of both our

families had gathered for a huge farewell picnic. We found ourselves lost along the way, having gotten fouled up in a parade, and
arrived at the scene of the picnic to find everyone well oiled and
having a glorious time. More pictures, more questions and lots
more wisecracks. The photographer and the reporter were in hog
heaven. He threw his cameras around with great aplomb.

My niece, Heather, had made an enormous cake in the shape
of a bus, all decorated with names and roses. One sister-in-law
gave us a large box of baklava to eat on the way. One brother,
mine, gave us some more whiskey, "for snakebite," and one friend
brought a wreath of flowers to decorate the engine of the bus. The
children, and there were many, each with his or her favorite
cousin spent three wild hours clambering over the huge rocks that
gave the park its name. The littlest ones all played happily
together in the woods. The grown-ups stood around laughing and
chatting and drinking while some of them tried to climb the
rocks, too. One darling man, the father of one of my friends,
whispered that, "If you run out of money, just wire me and I'll
send you as much as you need. All you'll have to do in return is
come and talk to my Rotary Club about your trip." Wasn't he a
love? He also gave us ten steaks for our first night's dinner, bless
his old Rotarian heart.

As the afternoon turned into evening, it occurred to every
one of us that it might be years before we saw each other again;
the good-byes began and continued through several more bottles
of wine. At long last, as the relatives began leaving, we decided it
would be much wiser not to try to make Vermont that night and
Jack went off to consult with the caretaker. That worthy gentleman said, "Well, since the season hasn't really started yet, and
since there isn't anyone around anyway, you might's well camp
right down there in that there campsite, which hasn't really
opened yet." So we set up our first camp then and there.

Mike and Jon tried to act as though they had been setting up
teepees for years. Pete yelled at them and told everybody who
cared to listen that they were doing everything wrong and that

this was the way to do it. Finally, the entire pile of poles and canvas collapsed on them, much to their disgust and our amusement. Peter announced loudly that if they had listened to him in the first place it would have been set up by now, while Jon giggled and Mike picked up the poles and started to untangle the jumbled mess. Naturally, the photographer got the whole fiasco on film and the boys knew it.

*   *   *   *   *

Before we left on this wild trip to Alaska, we asked everyone to compete for a prize by naming the bus or the expedition. Several people made rude remarks about the mentality of people who drive five thousand miles with eight children, but some came up with suggestions:

Blunderbus   Omnibus
Yukon Sal   Sal's Safari

10 into 49 (ten people into the 49th state, get it?) and others that are unprintable.

My cute niece Maz won with LESH GO! and we awarded the kittens to her. My brother Bob had volunteered Leshpedition but he was a bit under the influence of the demon rum at the time, and if he had won, I don't know which of us he would have drowned, me or the kittens. In fact, now that we look back on it, we realize there was no great rush to compete in the little contest. I think we might have gotten some better names if we had not announced the prize ahead of time.

Anyway, the name is now written across the back of the bus, above the door, for all to see:

"LESH - GO"

Then I painted across the front:

FALMOUTH - FAIRBANKS
LOCAL

Ted Polumbaum/TimePix

*   *   *   *   *

Jack set up the lean-to over our kitchen. This was a tarp he fastened to the side of the bus so we could go in and out of the bus without getting wet if it was raining. The stove was unfolded and its chimney put through its hole in the tarp. A fire was made in it and soon our steaks were sizzling. We were trying to make the camp look the way it would every night on the trip, but since it was really our first time we were clumsy and frustrated. I tripped over the same tent rope three times and Tom fell into the water pail once. In our effort to look casual and practiced at camping, I got out the guitar and we all sang a song or two as the photographer clicked away and the reporter wrote furiously. And some of us can't even carry a tune!

Now, everyone has gone home. The photographer and the pretty reporter have left finally, and the little children are asleep. I wonder when, or even if, I will see my brother Bob and his wife Lois, or their kids, again. Just thumps and grunts are coming from the teepee, and Jack and I and the baby Tom are cozy in our small green tent. There is no sound at all but the peeping of the tree frogs. All the confusion and gaiety is over, as is the first day of this epochal trip.

May 23

I hate morning. Even in a nice warm house with everything all electric, I hate morning. But Jack just loves it. He bounces up and out of bed, full of good humor, whistles gaily as he does his exercises and cheerily goes forth to greet the day; while I grumble around and bang things. He was worse than usual today. So was I.

The night was miserable. It rained all night and nobody got wet but me. The tent leaked right over my head and a small, cold trickle found its way into my half of the sleeping bag. In the middle of the night, of course, I heard a bear. It was trying to get in the bus to eat the girls. I heard it doing that. I poked Jack and hysterically whispered into his ear that there was a bear outside and to be quiet. Since I was making all the noise anyway, he merely looked through the door flap and then laughed, "It's only a skunk. He's eating the cake." And with that he went back to sleep. That's only one of the irritating things about men; they can just go to sleep in the face of a thing like that. I gave up, retreated to the depths of the sleeping bag and hoped that nothing would startle that skunk.

So this morning my head ached just horribly. Wouldn't yours? All I wanted was more sleep.

After Jack got up full of enthusiasm for the life of the road, I burrowed down into the nice, warm bag for a final snooze. I could hear Jack pumping water and figured he was starting breakfast. The boys were stirring in the teepee, eager to be at this business of camping, so I drifted off to sleep again thinking this might not be so bad after all. The kids and Jack were doing all the work and loving it and I gloated as I thought of all my friends back home who had said, "You're so brave, dear."

Ted Polumbaum/TimePix

Then Jack called.

"Yoo-hoo! Are you getting up?"

"Of course I'm up." And I snuggled down a little deeper. Just a few seconds more.

"Because if you're not, I shall have to take steps," he added.

"Hm-m-m," I said. Then he started muttering under his breath. This was the danger signal. When Jack starts muttering, I move. But not fast enough this morning. All of a sudden the entire tent collapsed on top of me and I was left to flounder around with yards and yards of green canvas hampering every move. So when I finally emerged, half-dressed and un-groomed, I was as cross as two sticks and could only hope the tea was ready.

It wasn't.

Well, the girls back home were right, I am going to have to be very brave. I hate camping already. After all that talk about making this trip in a slow, leisurely fashion, here was Jack making us all hurry up. And it was only the first day. So I made tea and oatmeal and not enough of either. We filled up on baklava and carrot sticks left over from yesterday's picnic and, after this tasty, nourishing meal, we broke camp.

Broke Camp: Doesn't that sound professional? What happened was that everyone, including me, had forgotten just what he was supposed to do. While Jack was efficiently taking down our tent, rolling up sleeping bags, stowing duffel and, in general, acting as though he had done it every day of his life, the rest of us, with the possible exception of Mike, who is almost as efficient as his father, ran around bumping into each other, dropping things and picking them up, then putting them where they didn't belong. The younger boys lazily collected the dishes in order to wash them but hadn't thought to heat the water; Sally Ann had taken Bets and Tom off somewhere and had to be found; Pete and Jon forgot how to take the teepee down. It solved that problem by falling on them, and they just sat there muttering swear words and giggling. There just seemed to be a hopeless confusion of sleeping bags, wet bathing suits (now who went swimming and where?), air mattresses that needed to be deflated, axes, boxes with no lids, pieces of damp clothing and half-eaten dishes of congealed oatmeal.

Just as the confusion reached its peak, Jack started the motor. Absolute panic ensued.

Everything else was simply hurled onto the bus with complete disregard for safety or order. The girls, certain they were being abandoned, started screaming and running out of the woods with Tom in tow. When we all fell exhausted into the bus, Jack turned off the motor and got off. I thought, he's going to make a personal check of the campgrounds to make sure everything is aboard. I don't know who he thinks he is, I checked everywhere myself just before I got onto the bus.

He returned to the bus carrying a pair of sneakers. "Your shoes, dear?"

"Well, yes they are, but I thought I ... What? Yes, those are mine too ... Oh, that pan! Well, I guess I did leave it out of the trunk now that you mention it. Ha ha."

Maybe we'll get better at this business of camping as we go along, but I have my doubts.

*   *   *   *   *

We cruised out of Purgatory Chasm State Park at 9:00 a.m., still rattled from all the attention from the photographers and reporters, glad to be finished with them. I can only hope I don't look as old as I feel. While the kids played games or stared out the window, I did my household chores: put away food; put dirty clothes into the "washer," which we have not filled with water yet; made the bed. And, much to Betsy's delight, even combed my hair. She always sings out, "Mummy's going to be a witch now!" Sweet child.

We drove through Vermont today. My, that is pretty country. I almost wish we could have just stayed right there and never moved again: lovely, warm meadows, slim birches and sturdy maples. Somehow, that country is most appealing to me; it was with a pang that, as I gazed at it, I knew I'd probably never see it again. Alaska is so far away.

We stopped in a small town for gas and milk. When we pulled into the gas station, Jack asked the attendant, a laconic fellow who leaned heavily on the pump the whole time we were there, to "Fill 'er up with reg'lar."

The attendant shoved his hat back on his head and drawled, "Ain't none. Last feller took it all." Then he scratched his head for a moment, spat and, turning his back on us, went into the station. So there. We crossed the street to the competition, filled 'er up with reg'lar and off we went again.

We rolled along quietly, each person thinking his or her own thoughts as we gazed, unseeing, at the passing country. We planned to spend the night at an old farmstead, which at one time we had wanted to buy. We knew it had been sold but was still unoccupied. The roads had become narrower and bumpier since we left the gas station and got closer to Canada. Winters here are pretty severe so populations dwindle. Mike had taken the wheel so Jack could rest. The bridges crossing the rivers and streams became narrower also and it was on a very small wooden bridge, almost within sight of the farm, that Mike inadvertently stalled the bus.

We all giggled, but Jack roared off the bed where he had been napping, raging mad and shouted at Mike. Mike, who was too old to cry and too young to laugh, took the only option left, silence. Stony-faced, he turned off the ignition, stood up and with immense dignity walked to the back of the bus where he sat down on the edge of the bed and looked out the window. Jack, stunned by this show of independence and insubordination, strode to the driver's seat, turned the key and drove the last mile to the farm, shaking his head the whole way. It was one of those delicate situations, which arise so often in every family, when the only wise course is to remain silent throughout the whole affair.

*   *   *   *   *

Amadon Farm was as nice a piece of landscape as I could desire, one hundred acres of gently rolling hills covered with maple trees. Sugar maples they were, giving sap in the spring and glorious color in the fall. A small brook tumbled down from the mountains further north, crystal clear and icy cold. It ran through the springhouse on the farm, where it filled a stone pool for chilling the milk. The barn was immense — stalls for fifty cows and a hayloft large enough for at least that many children to jump in.

As for the house, it too was large, L-shaped, with eight or nine bedrooms in one wing, a big, airy kitchen with windows on both sides, and a woodstove large enough to cook for the many workers at sugaring time. The table in this kitchen could seat twelve or fourteen people from the sugaring crew or ten Leshes at dinner. Just off the end of the kitchen wing was a storage room for the hundreds of bright, shiny pails used in gathering the sap from the maples. We loved it. We had wanted to buy it and turn it into a ski resort to serve the new Jay Peak ski area, which was just opening.

May 24

It was a lovely place, quiet and lush. The twittering of swallows as they swooped around was the only sound I heard in the early morning. When I opened the flap of our tent, there, about twenty feet away on a small bluff, stood two beautiful fawns, ears up and long baby legs ready to leap away to safety. We just stared at each other, and then, when I blinked, they were gone.

I made breakfast, oatmeal and cocoa.

This farm pulled at me. "Stay here," it said. "Remain in these eastern woods where you belong. Live here and make maple syrup in the spring. Stay. Stay. Stay." The fawns had been an omen I thought, sent to convince me.

But the bus was packed. The children had finished breakfast and were staring at me. Jack was aghast. "Stay here?" he shouted. "Are you nuts? We're going to Alaska, remember?" Oh yes, I remembered all right. So I resolutely turned my face westward and the trek continued.

We finished packing up and drove down the road, across the little wooden bridge without mishap, and were soon heading north again.

*   *   *   *   *

Today we reached and crossed the Canadian border into Quebec. I had expected great flag-waving and fuss and bother, but the whole thing was accomplished without a flutter. We had ordered a pamphlet telling us what we could and could not bring across the border into Canada, and Jack, being the scrupulous person he is, adhered to the letter of the law. I had wanted to bring all sorts of home-canned goods along, but the leaflet said, in large letters, NO FOODSTUFFS, so I left it all behind. The agents never even glanced at the cases of jam and chutney I had packed — I could have brought cases and cases more.

The customs agents did have to see all the guns though. We had to wake Bets and Tom who were taking their naps right then, remove the mattress and produce the box of guns. It was pulled out and carried into the customs house where some charming uniformed men with divine English accents did all the necessary things.

* * * * *

Quebec is flat. The road is wide and lined on either side with tall poplar trees, carefully spaced. Fence posts along the sides of the road are painted red with yellow tops. Isn't that odd? But it is pretty and in all the cold gray rain it provides a welcome note of color.

The mailboxes are parallel to the road, not at right angles to it as they are in the United States. And worms must be the principal crop, judging from all the roadside signs that proclaim, VERS A VENDRE (worms for sale). This was not one of the phrases covered in Jack's French class so it was some time before we discovered just what was being sold.

* * * * *

It rained all day. It didn't really rain until we had broken camp and were on the way. It had just drizzled during the night and nobody got wet.

Betsy is taking this trip in a horizontal position. She takes frequent naps while we are driving and loves to go to bed in the bus at night. I hope it lasts all the way to Alaska and, I must say, I sometimes wish one or all of the boys would be affected that way too.

After driving for endless, bone-shaking miles over a bumpy road, we came to a small general store where we bought groceries, including some excellent cheese. We were heading to Quebec's Mont Tremblant Provincial Park to spend the night.

The entrance to the Park was guarded by a fence. At the gate across the road, we stopped and several terribly important looking men came over to the bus. They wanted our entire life histories, as individuals and as a family. It took some time; and the bored children got off the bus and scaled the cliff behind the guard-house. These officials were overly upset by this, I thought. And while they were being upset and Jack was trying to calm their fears, a car came from the other direction and pulled to a halt behind the gate. Always helpful, Dave opened the gate for them and they drove on through and away. The officials became even more upset by this, so we had to call all the kids back into the bus while the interrogation and inspection were carried out to government satisfaction.

The park has several campsites and we managed to select the one with the most blackflies.

May 25

After a very, very uncomfortable night, we cooked up a tremendous breakfast and prepared to spend the day relaxing and reorganizing. A breeze had sprung up, banishing the blackflies. Dave and Jack decided to take the canoe and go for a little trip downriver. I was supposed to meet them at the gate to the park, where they would disembark. Jack took the brand new camera someone had given us as a gift so that we could record our trip on film. And the two of them disappeared down the trail to the river, carrying the canoe. Just as they got out of sight, I noticed Dave had left his lifejacket on the picnic table, but they were too far away to hear me yell and nobody else was around to run after them. Knowing Dave was a good swimmer, I wasn't unduly alarmed.

With everyone occupied I set about my daily household chores; they don't change much while camping. Everything is harder, and I was in the midst of these when suddenly Jack and Dave reappeared, soaking wet and minus the new camera.

"Rapids," said Jack.

"Turned over," said Dave.

Later, and in complete privacy, Dave told me, "I was scared, Mum."

* * * * *

We drove and drove and drove, looking for a campsite. Passed two nice ones but, in our naiveté said, "Oh well, let's not go back. A really nice one will come along soon." So we drove some more and, finally, when we all could stand it no longer and it was getting darkish, we came to a pull-off spot on the side of the road that was a combination gravel pit and garbage dump. After a boring supper, we were lulled to sleep by the whine of heavily laden logging trucks racing by at high speed. I must learn to improve either my temper or my camp cooking.

May 26

Off to an early start. We are getting better at setting up and breaking down camp. The teepee hasn't fallen on anyone, and by now everyone has been assigned certain jobs so it all goes more smoothly. Bets' job, upon arriving at every new campsite, is to find the little house with WOMEN written on its door — her first spelling word.

The campsite we were aiming for was Esker Lakes Provincial Park, near Kirkland Lakes, Ontario, but due to very bad roads we didn't reach the place until late afternoon. Then the park road itself was thirteen miles long and full of ruts and rocks. But it was worth it. The park covers seven thousand acres and was perfectly lovely. Slim young birches and older dark pines are so beautiful together.

We set up our camp by the side of the clear green lake and spent a pleasant evening swimming, hiking and exploring. The total catch for the fishermen was one eight-inch trout. Each person's small spoonful was much enjoyed, in spite of the fish having been dragged around on a string, buried and tenderly washed several times by Betsy. After supper, a good one for a change, we put the canoe in the water and Jack and I spent a peaceful hour paddling around with a loon. We were the only campers in this entire seven thousand acres and it was a delicious thought. If this is wilderness, I'll take a double scoop.

May 27

We decided to stay here for one more day to rest up as well as to get some chores done. Mike tightened up things that had been shaken loose, and fastened down things that had bounced around too much on the rough roads. One of these was the potty. Having watched with horror, touched with hilarity, the antics of the girls as they poised, bare bottomed, over the potty only to have it skitter away as Jack turned a corner or changed speed, we thought it necessary to anchor it somehow. Jack did this very neatly. He braced it with small pieces of wood and positioned it back by the rear door, but off to one side in the stove space. He even added a handhold. I spent the day washing a huge pile of dirty, moldy-smelling clothes. We had not used the famous washing machine yet because it always seemed to be raining. Doing laundry was really kind of fun. The sun was shining, the children were happy down by the lake and the birds were singing gloriously. I sloshed around in the buckets and washtub, which we had brought along as a bathtub for the very young. I clamped the wringer to the collapsible sawhorse and ran the wet clothes through it; then hung them over the shrubs and trees where they all dried quickly in the hot, dry wind and smelled clean and fresh. As we have been driving further north we notice the lengthening days and tonight nobody went to bed before ten o'clock!

May 28

Off at 8:00 a.m. to drive back the thirteen miles of rutty, bumpy road. All the roads were so bad today that we had only covered 150 miles when we pulled into Greenwater Lakes Provincial Park. There is no one here at all: no caretaker, no campers, no one but us chickens. The water in the lake is a beautiful green and as clear as an emerald. There are large patches of pine pollen floating on the surface, another shade of green. Mike and Sally Ann seem to suffer with stuffy noses but the

Lesh family

pollen doesn't affect anyone else. The boys did not pitch the teepee tonight, last night either; instead they put up a tarp lean-to and a small pup tent. Our tent is so dry that condensation forms on its walls at night and drips down. Maybe that's what I thought was rain. It's wet anyway.

May 29

After a good breakfast of pancakes and maple syrup we packed up and headed out.

We drove into Kirkland Falls to do a large grocery shopping in a Dominion store, sort of the Canadian equivalent of an A&P. Jack bought a new camera to replace the one he lost on the canoe trip. Now we won't lose out altogether on pictures for our fall lecture tour. We found a Ford garage where we had the hand brake on the bus tightened, quickly, efficiently and inexpensively.

*   *   *   *   *

Ran out of salt three days ago and the meals have been pretty bland. We keep squeezing the saltshaker hoping for one or two more grains. We were happy to see a sign saying GROCERIES 4 MILES.

"Let's stop," I said.

"Whatever for? We just spent an enormous amount of money at that big store in Kirkland," said Jack.

"Salt," I replied. I really wanted to see the inside of the place; it looked homey and we always needed gas.

"All right, all right, we'll stop."

And we did. The store was a small, tarpaper building, which housed the post office, the grocery and the home of the proprietor and his family. What a cozy, pleasant arrangement, I thought, as we pulled up to the gas pump. They were all set up. So were we. Besides wizened apples and doubtful milk, I remembered to buy salt.

Endless miles of wilderness came right to the edge of the road. I suppose there is nothing but wilderness to the north of the road … south of it you'd eventually find the U.S.A.

Small tarpaper shacks appear now and then, close to the road, most of them sporting a four-seater garden swing in the front yard. The people can swing and watch the cars go by? Woodpiles here are as large as the shacks they keep warm. The children surprise me; the little girls wear frilly white or pink dresses and they run around in the mud in pretty white shoes and socks. The boys wear white shirts. And it isn't even Sunday. The roadway appears to be the sidewalk also, as we saw several families walking along in the middle of the road for an evening stroll. The little shacks are built on stilts or have high basements in order to cope with the spring floods, I guess. There are no screen doors that we could see. People lounged in the doorways, too, to watch the cars.

We camped at Klotz Lake Park, Ontario, thirty miles east of Longlac. I baked biscuits in the Coleman oven and they were delicious — the whole dinner was wonderful in fact. I must be getting better at camp cooking. It certainly is much simpler now, and lots more fun. There is still enough wine left so that I can have some as I prepare the evening meal and we can have some at every course. Maybe that's why it's so much more fun. After supper we all walked up to where Jack had seen some beaver houses and spent an hour watching the beaver. Also saw some otter slides! The children think that animals must have fun, too. The re-capping is coming off the left outside rear tire. Jack and Mike scare me to death when they go about fixing it, lying under the bus, as they must.

Tom was feverish yesterday but is all better now, which is a relief. I'm begging for a two-day stop soon so I can wash clothes again. There is a small mountain of dirty clothes in the aisle of the bus. Any hour now they will start to mold. I need to do wash or buy new clothes. The children get filthy, what with handling

Ted Polumbaum/TimePix

blackened pots and pans and just playing in the dirt. They have
encountered bloodsuckers for the first time in their lives and are
both horrified and fascinated by them. Sally Ann had one in a
can, which she was very fond of and wanted to keep as a pet. That

was all right with me until I saw her kissing the slimy thing, at which point I told her she had to leave it behind in the lake.

May 31

We left Klotz Lake at nine in the morning and drove through uneventful and uninteresting country, more shacks close to the road with their white swings in the yard and rotting cars alongside. Made camp in an equally uninteresting area called Kakabekka Falls Park. White-painted stones lined the paths and roads and the whole thing was very commercial and dull. We found a fairly isolated campsite and set up.

I was giving Bets a bath in the small basin because I didn't want to heat enough water for a proper bath when the caretaker suddenly appeared out of nowhere and said, "That your kid?"

"Yes."

"Put some clothes on her." And with that he walked off. The poor man has probably spent many a year enforcing rules and picking up tiny bits of paper, and hasn't much sympathy with the traveling public. I was just washing her and I can't very well do that when she has clothes on, can I?

May 31

Years later: Jack is one of those people who always knows what day of the month it is. He always knows where north is, too. He wrote the following entry in the journal.

Jack writes:

I can't figure out Sal's chronology. THIS is the date we left Kakabekka Falls with the goal of reaching Manitoba to camp, and we made it. Reached a provincial campsite on Falcon Lake in

Whitehall Forest Preserve, just inside the Manitoba line. What a place! Rows and rows of tents and trailers, closed up and battened down tight with not a soul in sight. These were seasonally inhabited camps, occupied on weekends, mostly during the summer months. Dreary beyond words. The tents and trailers were so close to each other that the tent ropes overlapped each other and we were given to understand that, on summer weekends, there were often a thousand people here. What a ghastly thought!

June 1

Sally writes:

Yesterday, we went about setting up our camp in the small space allotted to us. As we set foot outside the bus the mosquitoes started to congregate around us. They never stopped coming until we left; after all, they were used to a thousand people and now had to make do with only ten. We grabbed our head nets, which were conveniently stored in our cubbies overhead and pulled them over our heads. I thought everyone looked rather silly, but when I looked in the mirror, I stopped laughing. A girl shouldn't be caught dead in one of those things and I hope the girls at home never see me in one. Tom strutted around in his like an animated pup tent, small size. The net came down to his knees. He could take his supper bowl inside the net with him. But, at bedtime, his Blanky caused a problem; he couldn't suck it through the mesh. I told him he didn't really want it, but he did really want it, so I shoved the whole blanket inside the net and stuffed his arms in, too, where he could suck away, unbitten.

The rest of us fared much worse. Eating was a problem until we discovered that if we kept moving rapidly the mosquitoes left us pretty much alone; so it was an ambulatory meal and a most unsatisfactory one. We all went to bed determined to be brave about the whole thing, but it was no good. The mosquitoes had us and they knew it. They bit through the nets where the mesh touched the skin; they bit through the sheets, which we were using because it was much too hot and muggy for the sleeping bags; and when they found a tiny crack, they entered it in droves and bit and bit and buzzed and twanged. It was intolerable. After an hour or so of absolute misery, Jack leaped out of his covers, explaining that he was going to take the tent down in order to let the wind, which had arisen and was coming in off the lake, drive away the mosquitoes. He pulled at the center pole and, of course, the tent fell — on Tom and me. It was frightening. All the heat and mosquitoes and humidity were suddenly crammed into my face. I am normally claustrophobic so, when the tent fell, I began to thrash around in a panic to get out so I could breathe. This woke Tom, who started to cry. Jack was trying to kill both of us. Just as I thought I was breathing my last breath, filling my nose with mosquitoes in the process, Jack pulled the tent off us and you can guess what happened then; new hordes of mosquitoes found us.

At this point there was a brief thunderstorm. Up went the tent again to the accompaniment of strings of curses while, in the ensuing dampness, more mosquitoes were bred.

It was too much for Jack. He took off all his clothes, walked to the beach and stood there in the breeze off the lake, stark naked, but triumphant; he had won out over the mosquitoes for the first time.

He soon realized, however, that it was beginning to get light in the east. In order to avoid another scene with an overly zealous caretaker and being ordered to "put some clothes on," he was forced to return to the hot, stuffy tent and his hot, stuffy bed, not to mention the hottest, stuffiest wife in the whole world. We thrashed around for a while and could hear the boys slapping and tossing in the teepee, while the girls, in the comparative comfort of the bus and a mosquito net, were crying in their sleep. I decided to end the whole miserable experience and said, "What do you say we get an early start today and leave now?" Everyone instantly agreed. Although it was only 4:30 a.m., we leapt from our beds and, in another sudden downpour of rain and wind and thunder, we broke camp. Wet tents and tarps were thrown onto a muddy bus. Damp, sticky clothes were pulled on as we slapped, and jumped, and slapped again and again. In this manner we contrived to boil some water for tea as nobody wanted to bother with anything more at all, and we drank the tea as we walked around and around to keep the mosquitoes from alighting on us. Tom's little arms had managed to escape the head net during the night. They were covered with red, itching welts, which he scratched as he cried.

As the last wet sneaker was flung aboard and the last protesting child was shoved through the door, Jack leaped into the driver's seat, slammed the door shut and turned the key in the ignition.

Nothing happened.

Nothing. Not even a wheeze.

"Battery's dead." Jack wore the agonized look of a man going down for the third time. I could hear mosquitoes twanging and zinging away in fiendish glee as they thought of the hours of feasting ahead of them. On us. Before Jack could really get started at giving verbal expression to his inner feelings and thoughts, I hustled the younger children away. The older boys stood around, ostensibly to help, but actually to listen to this interesting flow of curses.

Behind all the stuff on the very lowest shelf was the battery, which that blessed Bill had given us back home. I have never been so thankful to anyone for anything, before or since.

Well, we finally got under way and, with great relief, opened all the windows to let the fresh morning air blow away all the mosquitoes that had decided to come along for the ride. We roared off down the highway in high gear, thankful that the whole damn thing was over, only to come to a slow, gentle but full stop.

Out of gas.

Can you believe it?

Jack, disgusted, put his head in his hands and didn't utter a word. Not even a curse. In fact, words failed all of us until Pete thought of the can of white gas that was to be used for the small gasoline camp stove. He climbed up to the rack and hauled it down and we filled the tank, cupful by cupful so we wouldn't spill any of the precious stuff, and it got us to the nearest gas station.

Which was closed.

So we just sat there, dismally swatting the remaining mosquitoes, and waited until the owner should decide to get up and open his gas station.

Two hours later he did. He was a very tall, cheerful man wearing knickers and red, green and yellow argyle knee stockings, a hand-knitted sweater and a gorgeous Scotch plaid cap over his red curly hair. He was a cheerful sight, and one that lifted our spirits considerably.

"Falcon Lake, eh," he asked. "Got bit didja?"

"Wait a bit," he said looking at Tom's arms and our red-splotched faces. He went back into the station, which was also a store of sorts, and returned with a bottle of calamine lotion. "Here," he said and thrust it into my hand. Then turning, he filled us up with reg'lar and waved us on our way. The sun came out and shone gloriously.

After a few hours the itching subsided and once again we laughed; even Tom giggled when I combed my hair and dead mosquitoes fell out. After lunch it was my turn to drive. Jack was having a nap on the bed, catching up on sleep he had lost during the dreadful night. I was wondering quietly to myself, why couldn't we do things like other people and go to Florida without the children, when I realized the engine was making a funny noise. I listened to it for a while, but the others are always laughing at me when I say, "The engine is making a funny noise," or, "I think the engine smells as if it needs water." I am sensitive about making any remarks at all about the mechanics of the bus. Suddenly, though, it began to sound loudly abnormal and, when black smoke rolled up through the floorboards at my feet, I knew for sure that what was happening was what I had always predicted would happen: We were about to blow up.

"Jack! We're blowing up! We're blowing up! Quick!"

Jack exploded off that bed, shouting things about people who didn't watch gauges, reached the driver's seat and turned off the ignition, which I, in my terror, had neglected to do. Yelling that I had probably burned out the entire engine, he tore open the door, rushed around to the front of the bus and threw up the hood. Then he disappeared into the woods. Mike did the same thing but without the bellows of rage.

As he, too, vanished out of sight into the woods I started to cry. "Well," I thought, "he's left me now with all the children and it serves me right." Then Tom started to cry. The girls joined in as the rest of the boys left the bus, one by one, like rats leaving a sinking ship. In order to straighten out their own emotions, they started fighting one another.

Of course Jack came back. It was either that or walk to Alaska. And, when the engine had also cooled down, he drove very slowly into the nearest town. Fortunately, it was the large town of Portage La Prairie and miraculously it had a nice, competent Ford agency and garage.

Lesh family

So here we are in Portage La Prairie, a one-street-wide dreary town. We are taking this opportunity to wash clothes, rest up and replace articles that have been left behind. Jim is buying a long-handled shovel to replace the one he left in the woods when he was digging for worms. Peter and Jon are chipping in on a new pipe saw to replace the one they left by the last woodpile a million miles ago. And Mummy is buying lots of greasy, ugly engine parts called, I think, bearings and rods. All those dollars I was hoarding at the bottom of the laundry bag, which were intended for fun expeditions and meals out, I heroically offered to Jack to pay for the awful damage I had done. He took them too. Well, it's the Rule we made before we left and I think I was the one who thought it up.

The highway widens as it passes through town sprouting a few narrower, side streets scraggled with homes. These roads, however, are straight and smooth, allowing endless cruising by the young drivers whose only obstacle appears to be the occasional visit from the law. A group of teenaged boys, with curiosity in every face tinged with disdain over our choice of vehicles, congregated to look us over. After discussing the roads and the weather and their accompanying dangers, one young man allowed as how, "If you can drive in Portage La Prairie you can drive anywhere." With that he roared off in the car with his pals.

*   *   *   *   *

Maybe it is a good thing that we are NOT making this trip by motel; motel owners are just not adapted to housing eight noisy, active children. While the bus is resting in the garage, waiting for parts, we are making fantastic arrangements for sleeping. We have taken a motel apartment, which consists of two small rooms with a double bed in each and a shared bath. That is, we not only share the bath with each other, but also with the occupants of the next apartment. It really is just a matter of remembering to lock the door while in, and to unlock it when out. This presents a problem to small children who have never,

ever, been allowed to lock a door. And the excitement of sleeping on a bed was so great that Tom, Bets, Sally Ann, Dave and Jim are sharing the bed in the room which opens into the bathroom, while Jack and I have the bed in the other room. Mike, Pete and Jon are sleeping in our green tent, which is set up out back by the washhouse. We have all had HOT BATHS and I spend every minute washing clothes in a real washing machine and hanging them out where they dry quickly in the hot prairie wind. Wonderful. Now that we are under a roof, with hot and cold running water, the sun is out and shining brightly.

June 3

Second thoughts on the night in the motel: I wonder what the tenants of the adjoining motel room thought when they came in late the night before last to use the bathroom? For, naturally, the kids had left the door wide open and the light on, so they couldn't help but see five children in one bed.

Work on the bus was finished yesterday at 4:30 p.m. so Jack drove it to the motel and we packed up, all clean and dry again, and climbed aboard. I counted noses and we were off. Determined to get out of this flat, flat country, we decided to drive all night. The road was straight and good, the night was clear and starry and I felt like driving, so I took the wheel after supper and everyone else helped Jack prepare the bus for emergency sleeping. That meant lowering the tables to bench height in order to make a bed of sorts for two more people. That made four. They snuggled Tom in with the girls on the bed and that left only three to sleep on the floor, head to toe. It was cozy and warm and soon everyone was fast asleep.

For some reason I was very wakeful so I rather enjoyed the drive across the wide, flat, treeless miles in the dark. A few days previous to this we had discovered how truck drivers manage to stay awake, and the knowledge stood me in good stead now. They chew sunflower seeds, which are sold in little packets at all gas stations and roadside grocery stores. It takes a good deal of effort to chew the kernels loose from the shells and then to spit out the shells. Your mouth and tongue get so sore from this activity that sleep is well nigh impossible. I bet those drivers "take things" too.

The gas tank was getting low, and so were my spirits when, along about midnight, I saw the lights of a town strung out in a long line across the horizon, like a string of beads. The prairie was so flat that, had I lain down on the road, the light would still have been visible. It was hard for me to judge distances in all that dark flatness and I thought the town looked fairly near, but it was almost an hour before we reached it, and I found myself dimming the lights long before it was necessary.

Glancing down at the dials on the dashboard, I noticed one of the wavery little needles was approaching a Red Area. I suppose your car does not have a Red Area? Well, I'll explain even if it is embarrassing. After that fiasco that resulted from my not watching the dials back there in Portage La Prairie, Jack had made huge red warning marks on the dials with a crayon. As he did so, he delivered a small lecture, which concluded with these words: "And, damn it, if a needle goes into, or even approaches a red mark please, for God's sake, STOP THE BUS AND WAKE ME UP."

So I peered more closely at that wavery little needle, but it was only a teeny, weeny bit into the red, and Jack was sleeping so peacefully I just hated to wake him. Besides, there was that big city up ahead with all the lights, and there would be a gas station soon, so I figured all would be well for a little bit more time. Then, when we got to a station, I would wake him and we could go in for a cozy cup of coffee, just the two of us in the quiet middle of the night.

After a few more minutes, the gas tank was registering EMPTY. Now that is one needle I do understand, so I pulled into the very next gas station that came along. It was closed. I could see another one a bit further down the road so I drove to that. Closed. I looked at the little needle, which had been just a little way into the Red Area and discovered, to my horror and chagrin, that it was now all the way in. Obediently, I stopped the bus and called quietly to Jack. He was barely awake when he said, "How long has it been discharging?"

"Oh! Is that what it's doing!" I asked with feigned innocence and crossed my fingers because I was about to tell a lie: "Oh, only a few minutes." His control was admirable. He merely sighed an enormous sigh and reached for the map. A consultation with the map, by flashlight, showed that we were close to Moose Jaw. It was just sixteen miles down the road so, with Jack at the wheel, we made a try for it. I crawled into my bag on the floor and went to sleep.

The next thing I knew, we were at a gas station in Moose Jaw, Saskatchewan, and I heard Jack and the station attendant discussing "that damn no-good generator." I heard this man say that there was an all-night mechanic a couple of blocks away and, after filling up the gas tank, we rolled off into the night to find him. We didn't make it. The generator gave up the ghost in a dismal alley we'd blundered into while looking for this all-night mechanic. It was between a junkyard and a gas refinery and since there was no time to choose the lesser of the two smells, Jack pulled over to the right, turned off the ignition and the lights and lay down on the only available space left on the floor. His head was on the foot brake and his feet were in Mike's face. Thus we passed the night.

*   *   *   *   *

It was a rather grim awakening; the smell from the refinery was overpowering and there was not one single bush in the entire junkyard for me to squat behind. We used the accommodations in the bus after promising each other "not to look"; then, unwashed and uncombed, we set off on foot to find a restaurant.

This was our first restaurant meal on the trip and we were not, in any way, prepared for it. We were all wearing the jeans we had slept in and I had lost my lipstick, but the waitress overlooked these infractions of dress code and brought cocoa, pancakes, sausage and cereal with a smile as wide as all outdoors. The boys were thrilled to be eating out and the prospect of no camp to break and no dishes to wash put everyone into rollicking good humor.

*   *   *   *   *

Jack located the all-night mechanic, who by this time had gone to bed, but who had an all-day partner. He and Jack went to work on the generator. I took all the kids and wandered around until we found a park where the young could play. There were swings and slides and a sandbox, so they were happy. The boys went off to explore and I sat in the warm sunshine and picked up my knitting. It was a delightful, relaxing interval but all too brief. The generator, that "damn no-good thing," was back in shape. Jack drove around town, picking up Lesh boys here and there, then back to the park for me and the little ones. All aboard once more, we cruised onto the open road, once again over flat, flat country.

One of Alberta's exemplary roadside camps was our destination for the night and we got there around suppertime. There was a large, log shelter, which contained an enormous woodstove and several picnic tables. The toilets were clean, so clean there was no odor, and that's saying something for an outhouse. Also, there was NO graffiti anywhere. And that IS saying something!

There was enough room for several families to cook and serve meals and several families were doing so. It was fun to talk to other women for a change and the kids all ran around together and had a good time. There were even some girls for the boys to smirk at.

People were fascinated by the teepee. They wanted to peek inside and seemed awed by the sensibleness of it; the way the smoke was directed upward toward the smoke hole, and the fact that there was so much room inside — room enough for the five

Ted Polumbaum/TimePix

Ted Polumbaum/TimePix

Ted Polumbaum/TimePix

boys and all their bedding. And by this time, the boys were quick and adept at setting it up, raising admiring looks from other campers, boosting the boys' spirits to the point of not quarreling among themselves. That was a real boon for the rest of us.

When supper was over and the dishes washed and put away, Jack and I took a walk over the rolling prairie. The late evening twilight was lovely; signs of civilization were soon lost behind us and there seemed to be no fences or boundaries all the way to the edge of the world. Silence surrounded us utterly except for the occasional lilt of birdsong and the bawling of an unseen calf.

June 5

Jack writes:

We had an uneventful trip across Alberta to Calgary, a much larger city than we expected, population 200,000. Yesterday, we stopped at a snazzy new shopping center on the edge of town where all the boys bought white felt Stetson cowboy hats. The region around Calgary is quite nice. The foothills of the Rocky Mountains, the peaks of which shine in the distance, roll around Calgary in smooth billows. Great grazing land. Cattle are raised here, also some wheat and some hay, by the looks of it. Oil is raised here, too, judging from the huge bug-like machines that dip their heads down into the sand and up again, over and over, sucking up the oil, we think.

Stopped for the night at Big Bend Provincial Park, about six miles north of Cochrane, a small town west of Calgary. The usual long, bumpy ride into the park gave us glimpses of the wildlife hereabouts: a dead cow, a great blue heron, cow skeletons, another dead cow, magpies and eastern kingbirds. Not very interesting to anyone but the boys, who wanted to examine every carcass. The road ran alongside a pretty little stream of crystal clear water.

Our campsite in this park was just beautiful and so was the weather. The tent and teepee were set up near the stream, which had numerous small waterfalls. There was an excellent playground for the kids and, best of all, a good cook stove.

While we were preparing dinner we met the Murphy family from Calgary who were there for a picnic with two of their three daughters and a girlfriend of one of them. Girls! After supper, all the kids went off to run all over the grassy hills then came back breathless and rosy to sit around the campfire, sing songs and roast marshmallows. This is the way I had envisioned the whole trip; I never thought it would rain as much as it has. It was still light at 11:00 p.m. when the Murphys said good-bye and drove back to Calgary and we went to bed, supremely happy.

*   *   *   *   *

Rainy all morning, today Sal and I took a jaunt up a hill across from the campsite while the boys were striking camp, then we took off in the bus for Banff.

Arriving in Banff, we drove around the town, which, in itself, is not remarkable, but the surrounding mountainous country and deep forest are spectacular. We inspected some highly developed campsites in and around town but rejected them all for a more isolated camp, Mt. Eisenhower campgrounds. On the way to this place we saw mountain goats, mule deer and black bears — no dead cows at all. Wonderful day.

June 6

Jack continues:

Had a visit from a bear last night, he ransacked the camp garbage cans and bit a hole in our "plastic washing machine," but otherwise did no damage. Mum was very brave the whole time he was here.

No travel today. It was cold, windy and rainy all day. Mike, Pete, Jon and I took a hike, eleven miles long, to see the Johnson Canyon Falls. We arrived back in camp soaking wet and utterly exhausted but recovered after a couple of hot toddies for me and hot cocoa for the boys. Jim and Dave later hiked to the same falls, but they got a ride to the trailhead so hadn't as far to go on foot.

Sally writes:

Now it's my turn to write again. Here is what I have to say about laundry at Johnson Canyon campground: Today I get to do the wash. In fact, I am doing it right now. Unfortunately, we happen to be in Banff Provincial Park, which, I am told, is one of the most beautiful places in the world. I say unfortunately because I am spending the first sunny day we have had in eons in this sweltering cell, trying to get the clothes clean. What I wouldn't give for my washing machine and dryer right now! Talk about the simple life, would I? Who needs a washer, said I? Well, dearie, I don't have one now and, if this is an example of living basically, the Indians can have it. Remember I told you about the wonderful garbage-can arrangement for washing clothes — about how you put the dirty clothes in it in the morning, along with hot water and soap? Hot water? Where do I get that? And how the motion of the bus as we drive along works like the agitator in a real washing machine, remember that? It all sounded so blissfully simple, didn't it? Well, it might work if we had cleaner children or sunny weather. We have neither. I tried it. I filled it up last Thursday, added cold water, there being no hot, and put some soap flakes in. Today is Monday and after four days the can is one disgusting, gelatinous mass, which smells vile. It took both Jack and Mike to get the thing out of the bus and into the washhouse. And here I am, stuck with it on this sunny day.

We had chosen this place because the Book marked this camp with an asterisk, meaning, "has laundry facilities." This "laundry," and I use the word loosely, is a very small room with a cement floor on the middle of which stands what the park attendant called a "real good little stove." After two hours of feeding wood into this monster it is red hot and so am I. But the water in the washtub on top of the stove is only lukewarm, so I shove more logs in. The other quaint articles in this laundry are a scrub board and a wringer. I will now have a chance to try out these articles because I might have to use them for the rest of my life. I have just discovered that, if I lie flat on the cement floor with my head resting on the pile of dirty clothes, I can escape most of the heat and steam in here. As it has started to rain again, I will just rest here until the wash water is hot. Rinsing will have to be in cold water if I want to get back to camp tonight.

*   *   *   *   *

It took two full hours to scrub, wring and rinse that mountainous heap of dirty clothes, and guess what? The rain is coming down harder than ever. I can't hang the clothes to dry in the washhouse because there's a large sign on the wall telling me not to. As I am a good New Englander with a frightfully alert conscience, I must go and find the attendant and beg him to waive the rules this one time since: (a) we are the only campers in the park; (b) we have nothing clean to put on; and (c) we will be leaving in the morning and won't hit another campground with a laundry for nine hundred miles. Which is no lie.

He let me! I strung ropes all over that miserable little room, hung up every single thing, made a roaring fire in the "real good little stove," and fled to the bus, just in time for the sherry hour.

June 7

Jack writes:

Brrr! Cold again but, at least, no rain. Too cold to arise early so got a late start for Jasper. Our late start was rewarded by seeing three elk on the roadside. We stopped at noon to have lunch and see Lake Louise. While we marveled at its beauty, the children had a wild snowball fight. Tom thought the snow was fun until his hands got cold. Then he started crying. Bets fell into the snow and she started crying, so we decided to have lunch and got out the Primus stove to heat the soup.

At that moment who should walk up to the bus but Mr. and Mrs. Alfred E. Walker from Falmouth! I was so glad to see someone from home that I almost cried, too. They were staying at the lodge and thought they saw a familiar yellow bus so stopped by to see if it really was the Leshes. After a short visit with them we finished up our lunch and went on our way.

Sally writes:

The lodge and Lake Louise were so beautiful I told Jack we should come back and spend our fiftieth anniversary here. Who knows?

Jack continues:

Our next stop was to be somewhere in the Columbia Ice Field. We drove along the fabulous Banff-Jasper Highway with majestic mountain ranges along each side of the road, the Bow River rushing over rocks alongside and occasional blue or green lakes. Especially striking was the view of Peyto Lake from the lookout point off the highway. It snowed in small spits now and then as we were driving.

Lucky us! We came to a very nice, new campground along the highway — no name on it yet — with a semi-enclosed shelter, which felt good in the cold evening. There is an excellent stove with an oven. Sal baked rolls, two loaves of bread and an upside-down cake. In fact the whole meal was special: green peas, salad, rolls, creamed salmon on spaghetti, and the cake. High living, eh?

The boys and I climbed up the massive tower of rock behind the camp to investigate a pretty little waterfall. Beautiful mountains in every direction from up there.

June 8

Sally writes:

We drove on towards Jasper National Park, stopping at every viewpoint to gaze in wonder at glaciers of blue ice, gorgeous snow-capped mountains, rushing streams of icy, crystalline water and waterfalls. Along the way we picked up three hitchhiking girls in crazy hats. They were waitresses at Lake Louise who had arrived too early to go to work so had decided to see Edmonton first. The boys were so happy to have someone new to talk with they all jabbered away at once. The girls appeared equally delighted with our stories of adventure on the road. We were sorry when they had to get off, and all waved like old friends to each other.

Jasper is a beautiful town surrounded by beautiful mountains. We're staying at Cottonwood Camp, near town. It is a highly developed camp but handy to fishing and hiking places. I wrote a piece for the paper back home and did the laundry in a real washing machine and a real dryer, while Jack took the bus to have it greased. We met several ground squirrels and loved them. And the chipmunks are so friendly they will eat out of the children's hands. Tom and the girls are enchanted: They walk around with outstretched hands full of crumbs, calling the chipmunks. One ran all the way up Tom's leg, jumped onto his shoulder and thence to a tree! The girls were fascinated but jealous. "Why did he pick Tom?" was Bets' remark.

June 9

Jack writes:

Still camped at Jasper but drove up to Medicine Lake to go fishing. The boys and I caught about a dozen rainbow trout from the lake using worms. Salmon eggs, lures and flies not effective.

While we were all fishing, Tom, back at camp, was still trying to catch chipmunks. He was running around and jumping up and down when a tourist stopped and said, "And what is your name, little boy?"

Tom stopped jumping, stood as tall as it is possible for a two-almost-three-year-old, folded his arms across his chest and announced, "My name is Armin Bink." With that he ran off to look for more chipmunks. What possessed him?

Sally writes:

While in Jasper we did not take a picture of Jimmy in the hot springs because: (a) it was seventy miles out of our way and (b) the water is 126 degrees, which would have cooked him. "But Mummy! I promised my teacher I'd send her a picture of me in the hot springs because we just learned all about them in school! Well… couldn't I just put my feet in for a second while you snapped the picture? Please, please, can't we?"

Sullen silence from Jim the rest of the day.

June 10

Since we wanted to see the Cariboo, which is an area of land in British Columbia, not a misspelled animal, we chose not to go on to Edmonton and thence to Dawson Creek, which is the usual route for tourists to follow. That left us two choices of routes to get us to the Alaska Highway: either we could retrace our steps and go back to Banff in order to take the Big Bend Highway through the Canadian Rockies; or we could take the Yellowhead Pass, known as Canadian Route 5. On the maps, this route was variously shown as a green line, which means Adventure Trail — so help me, this is true — or a dotted line, which means a footpath, or a very thin red line, which means Unimproved Road. I had a friend back home who had driven over the Big Bend Highway and, two years later, still had not recovered from the fright, so I ruled against that way.

"Anyway, this Yellowhead Pass is a shortcut," Jack said happily and confidently. That should have warned me; I have been on Jack's shortcuts before and they are just what any woman would expect, longer and harder.

Just before we turned off onto the Yellowhead we met two men who had recently driven over it and asked them what the driving had been like.

"It wasn't too bad," said one.

"Christ, Mac! Don't take that rig over that road!" said the other.

Jack chose to ignore this second remark and took the first man's optimistic remark as gospel. I just knew the second fellow was right.

The road, if I may call it that, was named after an early-day trapper who had very blond hair and used to bring his furs out by a trail of his own blazing. Later, when a road was thought necessary, the engineers figured he must have found the easiest way through the mountains, so they just made the blazes a little larger and took a bulldozer through. No further attempt was made to improve the road at all, and, since this is now early spring, of course it was muddy.

Ten minutes after we entered the road, I knew all my fears were founded in fact: It was a horrid two-rut road with no room anywhere for two vehicles to pass each other. For that matter, there was barely enough room for one vehicle of our size to go straight ahead! While the right side of the bus was scraping the cliff side, the wheels on the left side were on the rim of eternity. Each turn in the road was a hairpin turn around a sheer granite wall, and each time I just knew we would meet another car coming from the opposite direction. I was paralyzed with fright. I heard one of the small people who were huddled in the back say, "Why are Mummy's hands so white?" Couldn't she see I was holding the bus up? Sometimes the turns were so sharp that Jack had to go halfway around, stop, reverse and then go ahead in order to make it. The whole thing was a nightmare to me but Jack and Mike didn't seem to have a care in the world as they shifted from low gear to the lowest gear.

*   *   *   *   *

We started early this morning with only a cup of cocoa under our belts and were getting hungry. It was raining again and all our spirits were at a dead low when we came upon a clearing and saw a mirage. There, on the side of the road, was a sign saying RESTAURANT. A miracle, I thought. This can't be true.

But it was true. There stood the Tote Road Inn, a cute, brightly painted, little Quonset hut surrounded by thousands of pretty flowers, a minute speck of a lawn and all this enclosed within a white picket fence. Then the real miracle occurred: Jack turned in and stopped the bus. He does not usually stop the bus unless we are out of gas or for calls of nature, so this was a real surprise. And there was an outhouse, clean and brightly painted also, where, besides a roll of soft white toilet paper, there was an old, out-of-date Sears catalog so those folks unacquainted with city ways could feel at home. The inn looked like heaven and it smelled like coffee.

We all trooped inside to be greeted by a smiling lady wearing a clean, starched dress and looking like civilization. How could she manage this? How could she serve ten people at a moment's notice? There was no town for several hundred miles in either direction, no electricity, no telephone, no anything! She could and she did manage. She served us delicious hot cocoa, hot buttered toast with homemade preserves, cereal and coffee. The children loved it all and I was warm and content for the first time in days. So we lingered for more coffee and more conversation.

Suddenly I heard a sound. I turned around and looked out the window and sure enough, up the road, from the opposite direction came two logging trucks carrying enormous loads of big logs, which were not tied down. They had chains on the tires and were moving very slowly through the mud. Suppose we had not stayed for more coffee? We surely would have met them on one of those wicked turns and I surely would have died of fright.

"Just good clean living," remarked Jack as he paid the bill, "come on kids! Lesh Go!"

Ha, ha ...

*   *   *   *   *

Reluctantly we said good-bye to the Tote Road Inn and took to the road again. Same road only narrower and muddier and ruttier. It was awful.

Stopped for lunch at an abandoned farm or camp with several fairly sound log cabins still standing and others that had collapsed. It was fun to explore and wonder about the people who had built them and lived here. A small clump of daffodils was a sad reminder of lost hopes and dreams; some woman had planted those long ago and they were bravely blooming amidst the ruins. Off again after lunch and we drove that miserable road for more hours than I care to recall, but we got to Clearwater around 6:30 p.m. There we tanked up on fuel and food before heading into Wells Grey Provincial Park, British Columbia and thirty more miles of driving over muddy, rocky roads. At 8:30 p.m., after thirteen hours of grueling driving, we reached our campsite and set up the camp.

June 11

Jack writes:

Wells Gray Park has a number of waterfalls on the Murtle River. Dawson Falls, near our campsite, is shaped like a small Niagara. Standing a few feet from the crest, as one easily can, the power of the rushing water is very impressive. Downriver three miles, reached by hiking along a good trail, is Helmchen Falls, a most spectacular sight. The water falls 480 feet into a great chasm below with spray rebounding up to the top again and rainbows in the spray. An almost frightening sight when viewed from above but there was no good vantage point for viewing or photographing the full extent. Sal and I hiked in to Helmchen Falls with Mike and the three little ones. Tom made it almost all the way in and most of the way back. Good little trouper. The other boys tried fishing in the Murtle without luck, as the river was so high and swift.

The chief disadvantage to this campsite is the water supply — down a very long, steep hill to the river. Quite a walk back with full pails.

Sally Ann and Bets decided to "camp out" last night in a neighboring campsite, so they set up the pup tent and crept in, where they slept soundly until morning.

June 13

Sally writes:

I have a few things to say about Wells Gray Provincial Park. I don't think it is all that wonderful. Nobody else has appeared and we've been here for three days and nights. Nobody, that is, except the one time I was all alone in camp with the two littlest children. Jack and Sally Ann had hiked off to meet the boys, who had decided to leave us all and go fishing on some of the lakes in the park and were due to return to base camp this day.

So I washed my hair and puttered around camp doing nothing much when a whole truck full of men drove by, very slowly. They all wore gray coveralls and they all looked glum. Until they saw us. Then the grins and catcalls and whistles started, making me a trifle uneasy.

But as the truck rounded a corner I noticed that one of the men had guns strapped all around his waist and carried a rifle over his shoulder. They did not look like Boy Scouts, either. To me they looked like nothing so much as a truck full of thugs whose main purpose in life was stealing little children and murdering their mothers.

I dove for the bus pulling Tom and Bets in with me, slammed the door shut and fell into the driver's seat, ready for instant flight.

The truck drove on down the camp road and disappeared, much to my relief.

After a while I realized we were out of water, so I grabbed the two buckets and started off for the river. Every park has at least one drawback and at this one it is the water supply; the only available water is the river, which is in full flood and racing through the canyon with terrific force. In order to reach the river, you had to climb down an iron ladder, fill your bucket without having it torn from your hands by the current, then climb up again, carrying the full bucket. No mean feat for a strong young boy but quite another matter for his mother!

As I got to the halfway point on the ladder with my second bucketful, what should appear again, but that truck full of men. Grabbing both full pails, I started to run back up the steep road to the campsite. Damned if that driver didn't put that truck in low gear and follow me up the hill! It must have made their day; it certainly ruined mine.

When Jack got back to camp I told him the tale of the trucks, only embellishing it a little and he nodded and said, "Prisoners. The park employs them. You were perfectly safe."

Oh, yeah?

Jack and Sally Ann met the boys coming back. They were triumphant, having caught six nice cutthroat trout ranging in size from twelve to sixteen inches. We had them for dinner and they were delicious. Is there anything in the world that smells better than a trout sizzling in butter over a campfire? I had baked three batches of cornbread during the afternoon, after my water-getting, so supper was a rather grand affair.

June 14

We broke camp at about 3:00 p.m. because of heavy rain and headed for Bridge Lake, on a back road naturally, which was just as narrow and bad as the Yellowhead had been. We were slogging along at a snail's pace because of thick mud when we spied, in the mud ahead, a tractor, which had become mired so badly that the driver had simply walked away and gone home. There was absolutely no way around the thing. Have you ever heard of a tractor getting stuck in the mud? Nothing to do but back up a ways and pull off into a small clearing, and there we made camp. Up went the teepee, the green tent and the cooking tarp. Soon we were all crouched around the stove, eating canned peas and corned beef hash, when it suddenly occurred to both Jack and me that it was our wedding anniversary. And not a drop of anything to drink a toast — just weak, warm coffee. Well, I married him for better or worse, didn't I?

Lesh family

*   *   *   *   *

I think I have discovered a new disease. It is called the Camper's Crouch.

I have it. I haven't stood up in weeks. Stood up straight, that is. Oh, I've stood on the bus, if you could call it standing. It is rather like standing up in a small boat in a large sea. You stagger and lurch around, grabbing at things that are about to fall on you, or which do fall on you, and kicking at things that threaten to slide across the floor and bang into your legs. You don't really stand up, in any sense of the word.

As soon as the bus stops for the night, I leap out and go into my Crouch. The stove is only two feet high so I have to bend over to stir things, and with this stove you have to stir all the time or the food gets burned. The trunk, which holds the pots and pans, is set on the ground and I have to hunker down in order to get anything out of it. The box that holds the food staples is also on the ground and anything I want, at any time ever, is on the bottom of the box under several other things I don't want. If I want to mix up a batch of biscuits or cornbread, I must assume this ridiculous position because everything I need for the entire operation is at ground level. I never realized it before, but the invention of the table has been of more benefit to women than the vote.

To get the fire going in the stove, I almost lie in the mud; believe me, ladies, it is always muddy. Since you can't sit in mud, there you are again, crouching like an ape. When the meal is all ready, then I call the kids and they all squat down to eat while I, for once, get to stand. But it still isn't really standing up; if I don't bend my head it will touch the tarp and that will produce a leak.

Then there is another version of the Camper's Crouch, a lower form of the same, so to speak. You get it when you are going to bed.

First you have to crouch way down in order to enter the tent without a lot of rain entering too. It is rather like getting undressed in a lower berth on a train, only a few comforts are absent. Primarily, the heat is absent. It is always cold and damp so I have become remarkably adept at undressing underneath my coat. All I have to do is take off the sweater, the flannel shirt, my slacks, long johns, another sweater, socks and underwear. In a final, desperate burst I fling off the coat, grab my nightie, pull it over my head and plunge into the waiting sleeping bag.

Two hours later, just as I begin to warm up a little and become sleepy, Tom, who sleeps in the tent with us, wakes up and has to go to the bathroom. Guess whose job this is! When I get back into bed with cold, wet feet, it starts to rain. Last week the zipper on our green marvel of a tent broke and when it rains, it rains on me. On my face. So I must crouch way down in the airless depths of the sleeping bag and there we are again, in that awful position.

Other women have the Crouch, too. I see them at night, leaning over their campfires, getting smoke in their eyes and hair and burns on their fingers, and I just know that their heads ache and their backs hurt and, to a woman, each is wishing she was back home.

June 15

Last night when we were celebrating our anniversary in the rain and mud, I did mention to Jack that, when we get to Alaska, would he mind getting me a new wedding ring? The one I have on my finger is so thin I fear it will break at any moment. I bought it when we got married because I had the necessary eight dollars. That was eighteen years ago. He promised he would and thus ended our celebration.

Jack writes:

Happy Birthday, Pete!

It rained, of course, during the night, but this morning no rain, just overcast and cold. Forty miles of dirt road and then we started on the Cariboo Highway, finally heading north in earnest. It was a great temptation to turn west at Williams Lake toward

Riske Creek and Tweedsmuir Provincial Park. And it also was tempting to stay on here for two weeks in order to see the Williams Lake Stampede. But I kept a tight grip on the steering wheel and, after washing clothes in a laundromat, we drove another twenty-five miles north to McLeese Lakes. There we stayed at a commercial campsite with trails and a motel camp, not very attractive, but okay. A windy and cold night, so not much fishing attempted but, in spite of the temperature, the boys took a short swim, only because some girls were swimming and they would not be bested. Pete's birthday dinner: hot dogs and beans, salad, birthday cake and fresh strawberries.

I discovered that the zipper on our green tent is no good; the slide doesn't close the zipper tightly.

Sally writes:

Well, I've been complaining about a wet face every night; does he think I am joking?

All the towns we have stopped at during this million-mile spree have been explored by the boys. Jack and I don't have a chance. I sit in the laundromats and watch the clothes swish around in the washer and Jack sits in garages and watches his dollars swish from his pockets to those of the mechanics who labor over the bus engine. The last time it was an exhaust manifold. This time it is an engine mount. I understood Jack to say that this is a thing that holds the engine in place. Since we have lost one, I presume the engine will fall out onto the road at any moment. And if that happens, we'll just take the wheels off and stay there.

*   *   *   *   *

I must tell you about the stores up here in the Great Northwest. They appear infrequently along the highway and nearly every one of them is also part cafe, part gas station and part home. So when you stop for gas it's a real occasion, both for the traveler and the storeowner. You can wander around among the shelves with a cup of coffee and a doughnut, pick up the groceries you need and chat with the owner while she is getting her dinner or ironing the clothes. Once, when we stopped along about nine o'clock at night, we were sitting at the counter with the usual cup of coffee, when a young voice sang out from a backroom somewhere, "Mom! Will you come and wash my back?"

I think I am catching on to the lure of the North for men; I really think I have the secret. Every place we have stopped for gas or coffee or groceries has been run by couples that have strikingly similar occupations. The man sits outside on a chair or a box, anything at all that resembles a sitting place. And he is telling the most wonderful yarns you've ever heard. Stories about bears, storms, floods, hunts and fishing trips roll out of him, each more fascinating than the last. How exciting, you think. What a marvelous way to live, you think. This is why we came up here. But where is his wife? Well, someone has to do the chores, you know. So she is making the coffee, and the doughnuts, since there are no bakeries for a million miles. And she is stocking the shelves, and she is working the gas pumps and wiping the windshields, and she is washing her kid's back while her old man just sits there and spins his yarns. Remember this, gals, when your husband gets the urge to Go North, let him go. But you stay home.

June 16

There is one constant about camping: Things could always be worse. And for that matter they usually are. If it is raining, say, it could also be cold. Or, if it is cold, there also could be wind, or mosquitoes, or floods in the tent or under the mattress. Or the wood won't burn but will smoke; or there's no butter at all and possibly no bread either; or the tent could blow down; or you might, at any minute now, spill the last of the coffee onto the fire, thereby putting it out. Every one of these things could happen, singly or doubly, at almost every campsite.

Last night was a case in point.

In the first place, we were forced to drive for too long. When this happens everyone is in a perfectly foul mood and mine is the foulest. It was almost 10:00 p.m. when we reached our destination, which had been glowingly described in the travel booklet we were following as having the best fishing in North America and "breathtaking scenery." Well, the scenery that greeted us certainly did take my breath; all of it in one great disgusted, "Well!" The bus could not negotiate the yawning ruts in the black, slimy mud, which led to a bottomless morass labeled PARKING. We had to drive clear around the lake and come in by another road, which was merely a narrower, yawning rut, which not only skirted the lake which had the "best fishing in North America," but which ran in and out of it in a whimsical manner. I was so scared I got out and walked. Then I became more scared as I watched the bus lean precariously to one side with all my children inside.

When we arrived at the tenting area, we saw nine other tents and their attending cars, all pitched and parked on a small gravel spot near the water. Squeezing that enormous bus, the teepee, our tent and the cooking lean-to into the remaining space was quite a feat but we managed it somehow. Looking over the arrangements for cooking, I threw up my hands and all but burst into tears. The fireplace was under water and the wood, which had been stacked nearby, had floated away out into the lake. And it was raining again. I predicted glumly that by morning we would all be under water and who could care less? Then I discovered we had run out of whiskey. And sherry. Well, I put on my brave Girl Scout front and said cheerily, "Let's all get busy and gather wood and we'll have a roaring fire in no time." I thought I heard snickers from the other tents whose occupants had gone to bed, but I ignored them. You know what? We were above timberline! There was not one tree, shrub or bush in sight in all that gray, wet, cold wilderness. So we had cold, canned corned-beef hash and canned figs. And there were ten of us and we were all tired and hungry. Peter gallantly announced that he would catch lots of fish for breakfast in the morning. This brought more snickers from the other tents, and we all crept into our cold, damp bags and so to bed.

But not to sleep. The wind had risen and was blowing hard, driving the rain into any crack it could find and I just knew the tent would blow down. It was billowing and creaking and flapping and sure enough it did blow down. But I was ready! I grabbed the center pole just seconds before the whole thing blew away into the lake. Jack crawled over me to put on all his rain gear, carefully fastened it snugly around him, unzipped the zipper and vanished into the night to find stones to anchor the tent. I was left in my pink nylon nightie, holding on bravely to that damn center pole and trying to keep Tom from drowning in the rain. I felt like the boy who held his finger in the hole in the dike, and I hated every minute. By the time the tent was secured against the wind, I had made up my mind never, never, never to be lured out of my house on another camping trip. Then Jack re-entered, dropped his muddy boots and wet raincoat on me by mistake, and crept back into our sleeping bag, as cold as a corpse.

This morning it was worse. The rain came down harder than ever and the wind had risen still more. So had the lake. Peter had overslept and had not caught any fish and there was still no butter, or bread to put it on. So we had yet one more breakfast of tea, which we made on the gasoline stove and drank standing up, there being no dry spot to sit on.

Most of the time though, we do have fun, and people along the way are curious to know just what a typical day is like.

*   *   *   *   *

Well, you know how it is, each day has its good moments and its bad ones. With large families, these moments often over-lap, while half of the family is going into gales of laughter at something, the other half is crying. After several weeks on the road, we still have not got this business of breaking camp organ-ized yet. The whole thing resembles a tornado that has lost its vortex, with everyone checking the campsite for forgotten articles. In spite of that, everything does get put back on the bus; Jack takes the driver's seat; I count noses and we chug on out to the road. The roads, which lead into and out of every provincial park in Canada, as well as those into and out of the state parks in the United States, are long, bumpy and usually twisty. I hate to drive on them so Jack or Mike gets to take the first stint at the wheel. Besides, I have all those nasty little chores that need to be taken care of daily: the wet, slimy dishrag must be wrung out of a window; ten pairs of sneakers, wet and dirty, must be paired and counted; the raincoats have to be hung in such a manner as to dry out without dripping on anyone; yesterday's blue jeans, also wet and dirty, have to be hung so they don't flap in our faces, but do get a little drier; plus the countless other little jobs that go to make up this mother's morning. Every mother in the country knows what this means so I won't go into details. I will just mention, though, that on a moving, swaying bus full of moving, swaying children everything is harder. Everything is always under something else, too.

When all the chores are done, we all sit down and look out the windows — for perhaps ten minutes.

Then a young one needs to use the potty. This starts a chain reaction until all three are done. One of the boys gets a book, another gets out a game and they all bump into each other and me. They always bump into me. And they fight and wrestle; push each other off the bed; drink cups and cups of water; fight some more; swing from the luggage racks; shout at each other and change seats. The water drinking, of course, engenders its own eventual problems. All of this wild activity is accompanied by small talk. Only, the talk is not small. Every word is yelled over the noise of the lurching, roaring bus.

"The elevation here," from the driver's seat, "is two thousand feet above sea level."

"Mummy," Sally Ann announces, "my scab is coming off."

"And," from the driver's seat again, "the population is 380."

Ted Polumbaum/TimePix

"Mummy," says a small and, to my trained ear, urgent voice.

"The floor back here is hot, Dad," from where Jon is lying on the floor and, of course, he is hot since he is on the floor directly above the muffler.

"Hey! Lookit the train! Lookit the train! Whooooooo... whooooo. Lookit the train!" Small Tom has seen a train.

"Mummy, I said my scab is coming off." She is speaking louder now because I didn't answer her the first time.

"Oh look!" Jack is yelling again. "There's a bird. I think it's a kind of a ... will you get the bird book, please?"

"Mum. Mummy," the small urgent voice is back, more urgent and less small.

"It had a white back and a reddish sort of neck and pointed tail feathers," Jack swivels around in the driver's seat to see if I am looking it up. I'm not. I'm watching the road. Somebody has to.

"The floor back here is very hot."

"Here comes the train! Whooooo ... Whooooo."

"Mummy!" Sally Ann's voice has, by now, reached a piercing screech. "Look Mummy! My scab came off! Look Mummy! My scab came off and I'm giving it to you."

"Mum." A new voice. "If I write a letter to Billy and send it tonight in whatever town we come to, and if it goes out tomorrow, and if he answers it two days after he gets it, do you think I would get it in Dawson City when we get our other mail?"

"The floor back here is hot as anything, and if Dad doesn't care, then we can all burn up, but it won't be MY fault."

"What did you say, dear?" I finally get a word in but everyone thinks I am answering him or her.

"I said, THE FLOOR BACK HERE IS HOT."

"I said, I think its legs were yellow."

"Mummy!" the small voice is now a desperate wail, "will you please undo my buttons?"

All this goes on and on, until the children begin to tire and drop off to nap, two on the bed after a short skirmish to determine whose turn it is to lie on the outside this time. The rest just drape themselves any old which way on the seats and look martyred.

The ensuing peace and quiet is so pleasant that we too are lulled and dulled and soon must stop to change drivers.

Instant pandemonium: Everyone wakes up and makes a wild dash for the woods. All that water drinking, naturally. Then the frantic rush back to the bus. Dad may drive off and leave us; who could blame him? And the fighting begins again because it is now someone else's turn on the bed.

Along about ten o'clock, only two hours since breakfast, the first pangs of hunger are felt.

"When do we eat?"

"I'm starving."

If I am driving we soon stop because I am a peace-at-any-price girl and just hate to listen to the whining. If Jack is driving he merely clouts the nearest whiner on the head and keeps on driving.

Lunch stops are usually fun. The menu is always the same for simplicity's sake and takes little or no preparation. If the weather is fine but hot, we make instant lemonade and accompany this with cheese, crackers, dried fruit and a piece of candy. This makes a quick, small, nourishing meal and seems to be sufficient for our inactive days. If the weather is fine but cold, we make a small fire and whip up some instant soup, either dried or canned. Everyone has his own plastic cup in his overhead cubby and is responsible for taking it off the bus at lunchtime and returning it to its place, clean, after lunch.

If the weather is just too awful to eat outside, Jack gets out his wee Swiss camp stove and we just make our soup inside the bus and sit around the tables all warm and cozy, while the storm rages outside. I am certainly glad we thought of traveling by bus.

The afternoons, as well as the mornings, are spent driving for, after all, we do have five thousand miles to go. About 4:30 p.m. we start looking for a place to spend the night. Sometimes we have a specific destination, which we have read about in our little travel book, but mostly we just stop at the first good spot we see. In fact, we always stop at the first one we see, regardless of whether it is good or bad, for the next one may be four hundred miles down the road.

Actually, the search for campsites has been quite simple. We aim for a provincial park and, after driving into it over a twenty-mile-long rut, which is called an access road, we drive all around the camping area to choose our site. The decision to stay or not stay is made by all of us. The inquiries made of the caretaker go something like this:

"Is anyone catching any fish?" This from Pete.

"How far do we have to go for water?" from Dave.

"I hope the wood is already cut." That's Jim.

"Where is the WOMEN'S?" ask Bets and Sally Ann.

Jack wants scenery and a spot as far away from other campers as possible, while I look for a nice, safe place for the little ones to play where they could be seen but not heard. If the answers to all our questions are satisfactory, we set up camp.

The alternative, getting back on the bus and driving any more miles, is too grim to even consider, so we always stay. Mike and Pete erect the teepee, by now a smoothly moving operation, taking about twenty minutes. The weather has been so warm that they have not built a fire in the center, but it can be done, very simply and effectively.

The younger boys take saws and axes and soon have a large pile of firewood for the stove. They find the water supply and fill the buckets. I start the fire in the stove, which the boys have set up for me, and think about dinner. Jack sets up our green tent and the girls return with a report on the location of the WOMEN and MEN signs.

At this point every child simply disappears. So far we have never asked them where they go. Instead, I get out my cut-glass wineglasses, which are carefully packed every morning in the double boiler, and Jack and I have ourselves a spot of sherry.

June 17

Got to Dawson Creek late today and decided to spend one more night in a motel before hitting the Alaska Highway, which starts here. The mud is appalling and the rain and cold persist. Tomorrow we will pick up mail and have the bus checked at a Ford agency. We decided to have one last night of hot baths and warm, dry beds. Not to mention clean clothes. We found

Ted Polumbaum/TimePix

McCutcheon's Motel and took two adjoining units, each with a double bed and a studio couch. Jack and I and the three little ones stayed in one unit and the five boys had the other. They called it "the bunkhouse" in true Western style but Dave's bunk was the floor. Tough to be the youngest of five brothers. They did their own cooking there and we heard a lot of giggling and smelled a lot of burned food. By the time Jack and the three kids in our unit had their baths it was my turn, but by now there was no more hot water. And there you are.

June 18

This morning we took the usual touristy picture of someone standing in front of the Mile 0 milepost. Then collected our mail, bought groceries, and while I washed clothes at a laundromat, Jack took the bus to be fixed. This time it was a broken strut on the exhaust manifold. I gather that now there will no longer be loud noises and backfires as we drive. That will be nice.

By noon the bus was fixed. However, something went wrong with the laundry; the dryers didn't work. I had to drape or hang every single article in the bus, where they swayed and dripped all day. Things were never like this at home. We collected the kids and, after counting noses, we were off on the Alaska Highway! It really was a thrilling moment.

The first few miles of the highway, or the Alcan as it is called, are paved and guess who was driving that part? When it was my turn to drive, I hopped into the driver's seat, rarin' to go. The country was flat, the road was good and everyone was happy.

ONE mile later the pavement ended and the construction began. I couldn't believe it. The road was horrible. Just horrible. Piles of dirt, soft and boggy, filled the road and, thanks to the everlasting rain, it had turned to thick mud. The road has a high crown, which encourages sliding off it into the deep ditches alongside and, in several places, we could see where this had happened. The worst was a tandem tank truck. It had broken in two and each half had been flung into opposite ditches. The driver and his pal were standing around, laughing and cracking jokes with the police. So we just drove by. I was aghast.

We stopped at Mile 143 for the night. Each mile on the Alaska Highway is marked with a numbered milepost, which makes knowing where you are very easy. Mile 143 was advertised as a Free Campsite and it was inexpressibly dreary. As we all filed out of the bus in our raincoats, Sou'westers and rubber boots, a lady in a filmy blue dress came up to me and asked how I had known enough to bring raingear. Aren't people wonderful? The kids all chickened out, saying they would rather sleep all cramped up in the bus than in that sea of mud. I was willing to join them, but Jack gave me a look that clearly said, "quitter"; so I said nothing but helped him set up the green tent. It was now that I wished our tent had a floor in it. Sleeping on mud was a new experience, and not a nice one. Those girls back home were right; I am brave.

June 19

We had a late start today because of a baby.

As we cleaned up after breakfast in order to get traveling, a young couple wandered into our camp. The woman was carrying a very small baby who did not look healthy. All three were gray and tired. Somehow they had found out that Jack was a doctor and had brought this small scrap of humanity for him to examine. The mother thought the baby had an umbilical hernia and wanted reassurance that she was doing the right thing. Jack unwound yards of gray rag from around the baby's middle, removed the fifty-cent piece that was holding the umbilical cord in place, washed the tiny tummy and put on a clean bandage.

The young man introduced himself as J.T.; no surname was offered and the mother remained unnamed. J.T. was a talker so we spent several hours drinking coffee and listening to him. He told us he had a cabin on the Kenai Peninsula and, as he was going "outside" for a couple of years, we could have the place to live in if we had a mind to, while we were looking for something permanent. He was full of information about Alaska. He told us how to fix joint weed so it was good to eat; how to smoke salmon; where to shoot a moose if you wanted to kill it (why else would anybody want to shoot a moose?); and how to apply for a homestead in Alaska. Homesteading in Alaska, he told us, is quite different from the Homestead Act, which is used in the rest of the United States. He went on to tell us where his tools were buried and where his cache was in case we should need any food staples. He ended up his informative talk with a sales talk that resulted in Jack buying his Mauser, which brings our total of guns to six. When are we ever going to use six guns? We were thrilled to have met a real Alaskan and sorry when our conversation ended and they and their miserable baby left for their trip "outside," which is how Alaskans designate the rest of the United States.

It seems we drove endlessly today — no place to stop anywhere. A person would make a fortune up here by providing campgrounds or motels, or both. Finally, we flagged down an oncoming truck and asked the driver if there were any pullouts ahead, and he told us about one. We continued on until we found it and drove in. As we went over the bump at the entrance to the clearing, we scraped off the spare tire, which was mounted underneath the bus. Also we broke the exhaust pipe. This necessitated a complete rearrangement of the interior of the bus to make room for the spare tire. Things are pretty crowded now.

June 20

Glorious blue-sky day and we were on the Alaska Highway still rolling along in high gear on a fairly good surface for a change. No mud or rain and no potholes either. In short, a spectacular day. I was driving and singing along with the tires, the kids seemed to be occupied with something other than fighting or shouting, and Jack was watching the world roll by. Along about lunchtime we saw a sign by the side of the road: Toad River, One Mile. Did I have any presentiment of what was about to happen? Did my sixth sense kick in to say, "Here goes lady; get ready"? No. I was intent on finding a nice spot to stop for lunch and hoped that there would be a pullout at Toad River.

The open rolling country was beautiful and, along with the blue sky, beckoned to us to come on out and enjoy it. Then I saw the log cabin. Even from a distance it appeared to be sinking into the earth. Beside it the Toad River rushed over gravel and rocks, the whole scene resembling an Alaska postcard. There was no driveway, just stony open ground in front of the cabin, which looked deserted. I pulled in and parked the bus for a closer look. It was indeed deserted. No barking dogs, no signs of children, not even fresh footprints. The windows were boarded up and the sod roof was covered with grass and tiny pink flowers. The entire bottom round of logs was sinking into the sandy soil and the whole log structure was weathered to silver. A bit like a little old gray lady wearing a flowery hat, I thought. It was so inviting and we had been sitting so long that I opened the door and let the kids run out.

While the boys leaped over rocks and, shouting with joy, ran off to explore the upper reaches of Toad River, the younger ones, already barefoot, ran to play in the shallows near the cabin and bus. I wandered around the yard in order to keep an eye on them while Jack, taking notebook and pencil with him, walked purposefully toward the log cabin. This, after all, was what we had been looking at in our mind's eye for the two years as we pre-pared to come and build a similar dwelling for ourselves. Here was a golden opportunity to examine one firsthand.

He could not enter, as the door was fastened with no less than three large, rusting padlocks; so he had to be content with examining the outside only. He walked around the cabin again and again, measuring, counting logs and windows — only two of these, and small at that — peering under the eaves to see how the roof was constructed and occasionally kicking a log, much as he might kick the tires of a car. All the while he was jotting down numbers and remarks on his piece of paper. There was a lot of head scratching and several times I saw him shake his head. Not a good sign.

During his inspection tour, I was daydreaming about living right here. It was so beautiful, so quiet, yet it had such possibilities: We could buy it and run a little store or restaurant or something. I was just getting to the part about what to cook and what to wear — a white apron was imperative —when Jack, back from accessing the fundamentals of log cabin building, broke into my daydreams.

"I don't know," he said, "if we can build a cabin this year. By my reckoning and from what J.T. has told us, if we had started a year ago to find land, sold the house in Falmouth, done all the paperwork, cut down trees — there are thirty-five logs in this small cabin, for starters — stripped the bark, sawed the logs to size and then put the building together, we might, just might, have been able to move into it this fall. And look at the size of it."

I looked and all illusions fled. What I saw was not a well-built, comfortable log cabin of a size fitting for a family of ten, but a miserable, sagging one-story cabin that might be useful as a barn for a couple of goats or chickens — but would never do for us.

He was right. It really was not much larger than the bus parked alongside and there wasn't enough room in that for all of us to sleep. I was too stunned to speak. Now what? I thought, is this the end of two years of our work and planning? I made a feeble attempt at humor, suggesting that we stay here, buy the cabin and start a restaurant.

"Where would the kids go to school?" Jack asked. "There's no room for study. What about laundry?" He had me there; what would I do at fifty degrees below with a frozen river? I guessed that it was the end of our dream. So, routine coming to the rescue, Jack sliced up the cheese while I made lemonade with the icy-cold water of Toad River.

The boys bounded down the hill, whooping and shouting exuberantly with long overdue exercise, and came over to join us for lunch. At once they noticed that something had gone wrong, so while they sat in the warm sunshine, they waited silently for some signal as to how they should act. Tom provided the welcome relief by falling into the river, which was only inches deep at that spot, and then crying loudly. He was rescued, dried off and wrapped in a big towel and set on a warm rock to dry.

Jack then repeated his litany about building a cabin and ended up his speech by saying that he guessed he could find a job as a doctor someplace in Alaska instead of living in the wilderness.

The news was received in total silence. Then Mike spoke up, "Would someone pass the lemonade?"

After lunch when everything was washed and put away we wandered around that pleasant place, subdued and thoughtful. I picked up a small black stone with white lines forming a cross on it and put it in my pocket as a reminder of where the road crossed over the Toad River. Whenever I hold that little stone, I will recall that enchanting place and the profound impression, a feeling almost like homecoming that swept over me. Its touch will remind me forever of that moment of reconciliation between fact and the disappointment that we will now be forced to change the direction of our collective lives.

As I drove out onto the highway, I glanced to the right; that way led back home, and for one anxious moment I paused. Then, turning left I said to myself, "okay, in for a penny, in for a pound," and once more headed for Alaska and whatever the future would bring. Mother never told me there would be these kinds of decisions.

*   *   *   *   *

Drove on dusty roads all day today. If it isn't mud, it's dust. Ugh. It rises in brown clouds behind every vehicle, and thank goodness there aren't many; it seeps into every crack and even gets into the food: gritty oatmeal, gritty cheese, gritty butter.

Stopped at Liard Hot Springs thinking it would be nice to wash the dust off and relax a bit in the warm water. The springs and bathhouse were quite a way off the road so we waded in black mud, called "gumbo" hereabouts, to get to the lower pool. Betsy and I hated it but nobody else seemed to care. The lower pool was too hot for the kids and the bathhouse was a revoltingly dirty, damp mess. I wouldn't let anyone in it. All the boys and Jack went on to the upper pool and had a hot swim and loved it. Sally Ann and I picked a bouquet of flowers, none of which were familiar to me, and arranged them in a jar on the workbench. We put the vase in the vice, which held it secure, and it looked very elegant.

Spending the night at Smith River. The rain has stopped, thank heavens, but I almost wish it would start again because the mosquitoes are so thick. On went the head nets and we all walked around eating dinner, picking dead mosquitoes out of our food and grumbling. The mosquitoes are worse than the night at Falcon Lakes, back in Manitoba. The boys all tried to get their heads under one mosquito net but it didn't work too well. They had decided that they would have to arrange their sleeping bags like the spokes of a wheel, with all the heads in the middle.

We could hear muffled remarks: "Would you move your elbow please? It's on my face."

"Hey move over — you're taking too much room."

"QUIT BREATHING, will ya?"

The cold night finally dispersed the bugs but Jack and I are tired of sleeping in a repellant filled tent and I don't think it is too good for the baby either.

June 21

We're spending this night in a Yukon shelter, four walls and a roof, windows and doors. It is cozy and warm and has a grand woodstove with an oven. I made a huge batch of biscuits. I've read and heard that the one thing most missed in the wilderness is bread, and now I can agree. Funny, isn't it, how you have to experience something before you can really believe it? On the highway we eat a lot of hardtack because the towns are far apart and the white bread in the stores along the road is too depressing and tasteless to even think about. Those hot biscuits, dripping with honey and butter, were delicious. We feasted mightily.

June 22 - 28

Have you ever heard of Atlin, B.C.? Well, neither had we, but when we saw a side road leading off the Alaska Highway, we just couldn't resist. It was the first side road we had seen in five hundred miles. After driving on this road for two hours through incredibly beautiful country, alongside the bluest, clearest lake I have ever seen, we came to a sign saying: ATLIN, B.C. Shortly thereafter we came upon the town itself. Its board sidewalks, false-fronted, gray-shingled stores and weathered fences had an air of desolation about them, as if they, and everyone in the settlement, were waiting. Waiting to "strike it rich up some creek," when the town will come alive again.

We knew from the guidebook that there was a campground someplace. To look for it we drove around the one block that comprised most of the town. It was around suppertime, the time of day when children are playing around near the houses, waiting for supper; but here, there was not a child to be seen in the entire little town. For that matter, there was nobody at all to be seen. Odd. After a bit, we discovered an open field that had a pile of firewood, a sagging two-holer and a fireplace. This, we assumed, must be the campsite advertised in the guide. So we set up our camp and planned to stay for a week or so, just to enjoy this gorgeous country and stop driving for a while. We are pretty near Alaska, after all.

Atlin, we soon discovered, is a relic of the Gold Rush days, sort of a living ghost town. Practically every soul is gray-haired and slow moving. There is Mr. Peebles, who owns a mildewy grocery and general store, and who wears his glasses on the very tip of his nose. And there is Mr. N. Fisher, who has "never made the trip to Telegraph Creek by air but lots of times by dogsled on the mail run." A wispy lady, whose time is running out, has a dry goods store wherein the stock is so ancient that even she isn't sure what's there. Then there is Mr. Greenjeans. That's not his real name. The children named him as soon as they saw him as he reminded them of some television character they had gotten to know during the three months we owned a set.

Mr. Greenjeans owned a six-room motel fairly near our campsite and he owned and operated a cafe on the same spot. The entire long building was painted dark green. He makes and serves two kinds of pie: raisin or dried apple, raisin or dried apple, year round. There isn't a choice, you understand. It is dried apple until that runs out and then it is raisin. Both are good and the boys love going over there to eat. They peeked in the windows of the motel one day and saw that the room they were looking into had been used. The bed was messed up and there were towels on the floor. The next room they peeked into was the same and so was the third. Room number four was clean and ready for a guest. We figured that Mr. Greenjeans just waited until all the rooms had been slept in and then he changed the sheets and cleaned the rooms. Sure enough, one sunny day, there he was in the yard with a huge pile of sheets and towels that he was washing right there. He had hauled his washing machine outside so he could simply empty the wash water, soapsuds and all, right onto the ground. What could be simpler? The boys helped him hang his sheets on lines in the brilliant sunshine, where they dried, bright and clean. Then he let me use his washing machine to do my huge pile of dirty jeans and socks; it kept the boys busy for quite a while.

Then there are the Norlands. Mr. Norland once owned a mine nearby and he invited our family to his house for an evening of pictures of the old days and, of course, the stories that went with each picture. About five young couples attended also, and by the time the evening was over, we felt like old friends. There was one old man with a long beard, who was buying up all the old houses and boarding them up. He was either an eccentric who collects log cabins or a shrewd old codger who knew something nobody else did.

We met Mr. Hasselby, who is a prospector. We'd seen his cabin in a ghost town called Discovery. A hand painted sign stood at what was once the edge of a thriving tent city; it read:

DISCOVERY

1898 Population   10,000
1960 Population   1

And that one was Mr. Hasselby. He invited all of us to come to his claim where he was still sluicing away up on Spruce Creek, "making good wages," and he laughed in a round-bellied, hearty way at everything. He has a fat, black retriever named Blackie, who waits on and worships his master.

Lesh family

At Spruce Creek he showed us how to pan for gold. The boys got a few flakes in their pans, convincing them that we were going to become rich by prospecting. Then Mr. Hasselby invited us to come back at the end of the week for "cleanup."

Back we went on Saturday to watch as he emptied his sluice box with a frying pan cut in half. In the end he had collected about five ounces of gold and gave Jack a couple of nuggets to be made into jewelry for me.

We were invited into his dark little cabin for coffee, made in a battered and chipped enamel percolator. Shelves on all four walls were crowded with glass canning jars containing nuggets and gravel from previous cleanups. During the winter months, when the snow was deep around his cabin, he separated the gold out with mercury, he told us, and then took it to town to be assayed and sold. An iron cot, neatly made with gray blankets, a small bare wood table, scrubbed clean, one wooden chair and a woodstove made up the entire furniture contents of the cabin. Snowshoes hung on the outside wall along with a pick and some gold pans. We were thrilled with everything we saw. He seemed a completely contented man — spending the winter with his trap line and his gold.

At one point we considered the possibility of staying there in that wonderful spot, but there were only thirteen children in the school, and somehow I wasn't too eager to become a citizen of Canada. There was a well-run clinic in the town, too, but having made up our minds to go to Alaska, we gave up that idea and concentrated on having a grand vacation, which we did.

Lake Atlin is very large — ninety miles long — and has the most beautiful cold, clear aquamarine water I have ever seen. And it tastes wonderful. The fishing, however, that's a different story. The place is a paradise for freshwater fishermen and, if the town never makes it on gold, it might do well on tourism. But I, for one, would hate to see tourists strolling up and down the main drag looking for gift shops.

Our kind neighbor at the campground, Mr. Sands, told us we could find watercress growing close to the road a short way out of town. We found the spot easily because of the bright green leaves growing in black water by the side of the road. The water was hot! The watercress grew in lush, green mounds of leaves. It tasted so good we picked bunches of it for supper. Betsy wanted to wade right in and have a nice, warm bath but when her toes touched the soft, black mud on the bottom she backed off hastily.

Lesh family

A small log house was rotting away by the side of the pool and we wondered who had lived there and why they had left. Mr. Sands told us the water stays warm all winter, even when the thermometer drops very low, and that the watercress stays green. What a miracle. Here in the frozen north where fresh vegetables are nonexistent in the winter, you can just pick fresh greens to keep healthy.

We hired Mr. Fisher to take us out fishing one day. It was a long eight-hour trip around the lake in his cabin cruiser with many stops to wet a line. Jon caught a lake trout, weighing seven pounds, and then Pete caught one that weighed six pounds. But Dave lost the largest as he tried to net it. A thoroughly delightful day and the fish were delicious.

On the following day we went out with Mr. Fisher again. He suggested we bring a skillet to cook our fish in, so I took along my favorite old iron one, and put a couple of lemons and a quarter pound of butter in my pocket, just in case. I also picked a heaping bunch of watercress to bring along. The day was perfect, clear and warm, with the water smooth as glass. We landed at a pretty little sand beach at the mouth of the Atlin River. While the youngest ones waded and played in the sand, Jack, Mr. Fisher, the boys and I fished from the shore.

We caught twenty-five grayling, cleaned them and soon had them sputtering over the fire. Never have I tasted such fish, tender white flesh with a deliciously delicate flavor. They were still wiggling when we popped them into the frying pan. We wrapped the remainder in wet cloth to take back to the camp.

We watched the water turn blue and silver and pink in the twilight. The evening was so quiet and serenely beautiful that we just sat on the beach knowing how lucky we were to have found this place, planting it firmly in our minds to hold against future troubles.

Lesh family

June 29

We hated to leave that paradise where we had had glorious sunshine for eight straight days, but felt we should push on. We broke up the camp, said farewell to our kindly neighbors, the Sands, and drove out of Atlin, past acres of meadows full of blooming fireweed. I have never seen its amazing bright purple color fill so much landscape. We headed back the way we'd come, to rejoin the Alaska Highway again. When we saw a second side road off the highway we drove into it and discovered Carcross. It is a small, very small, town. We watched a train come puffing in on a narrow gauge railway. A huge old steam stern-wheeler was pulled onto the shore after having made its last run many years ago. It was still in good condition, too. As we gazed at it, we wondered why it no longer churned its way over the placid waters of Lake Bennett. Later we found out that this stern-wheeler had taken on passengers and freight that had arrived by rail, and transported them to Tagish Lake by way of Mary's Lake. It was named the S.S. Tutshi. Maybe the roads had made it cheaper to move people and freight after they'd been built. But I think I would have preferred the boat trip.

Tonight we are camping at Mendenhall Creek with a lot of noisy Americans. I would rather have Mr. Greenjean's company.

We gathered mushrooms that we identified as morels. They tasted wonderful, a welcome change from canned meat, rice and beans.

June 30

Whitehorse, Yukon Territory. Whee! A city. We shopped, washed clothes at the local laundromat and ate ice cream. Jack took Dave to the hospital but nobody could find anything wrong. If he's not better by the time we get to Fairbanks, we will have him checked again. He's listless and dull and wants only to sleep. We spent a pleasant evening cracking nuts and jokes with a fat, jolly lady and her family as we all camp together somewhere along the highway. Her oldest son gave us a monologue of "a hillbilly at a football game," which was quite funny and had the boys in stitches.

July 1

We're spending the night at a campground eight miles off the Alaska Highway. We were amused by the antics of some beer-drinking Air Force boys. Sally Ann asked me, with some wonderment, "Mummy, are they big boys or men?" We tried to launch the canoe in the nearby river but it was running too high and swift, and both Jack and Dave remembered their last canoe trip. It's desolate land — eighteen thousand acres of timberland burned several years ago and the new brush is only a few feet high. Lots of homesteads along the way here because of the proximity to Fairbanks.

Dave has been sick for several days now. I wonder if it could have been the mushrooms.

July 2

We drove into Fairbanks in a whirl and, by way of celebration, drove straight to the laundromat where I dropped all our clothes and lots of dollar bills. Laundry facilities are sorely missed along the highway. But I guess it is an improvement over those available anywhere in the '20s and '30s.

One friend of mine who had traveled across the states from New Jersey to California when he was a boy in the '20s remembered that his mother had packed three trunks of clean clothing for her family of five, and had mailed them to various places along their route. One to Chicago, one to San Francisco and the last, to be picked up on their return trip to St. Louis. When they reached the first trunk full in Chicago, they unpacked it, repacked it with dirty clothes and mailed it back home. I think it might have ruined the trip just thinking about three trunks full of laundry awaiting the return home. So I shouldn't complain about the almost total lack of washing machines available to the public in this vast country.

Everything is dreadfully expensive up here in the Great North. While the clothes were washing I decided to do some shopping. What fun! I pushed my cart around, picked things up, glanced at the price, shuddered and put them back down. Whew! In the end, I walked out of the store with one bag of potatoes and a quart of four-in-one milk. That is concentrated milk: You add water four-to-one if you want drinking milk, two-to-one if you want light cream and one-to-one if you want whipped milk, which is sort of a substitute for whipped cream. It tastes like chalk water but the kids drink it anyway. Fresh milk is the one thing, besides bread, that will tempt them to behave, for a while.

Dave is still sick. He has been for a week, and by now I am convinced it was the mushrooms. We found a mushroom book and think we ate false morels, which can make some people sick. To think we might all have gotten sick or even died is too grim a thought to be endured. "What's done is done," as Auntie used to say, followed by, "No use crying over spilt milk." The lesson here is, as every good mycologist knows, if in doubt, throw it out. So Dave stayed on the bed in the bus while the rest of us explored Fairbanks. For these exploring sessions we had, early on in the trip, assigned one younger child to one older one. They called each other "my best-est" and the system gave Jack and me some much needed freedom. Usually, as I stated earlier, my freedom is spent in a laundromat and Jack's in a garage, but now that we are in Alaska the urge to hurry is not upon us. So we explored, too.

Fairbanks was not quite what I had expected, but then, neither is anything else in this great land. I had looked forward to a small town of log cabins spaced around wooden storefronts selling things like furs and candles and pails of lard. I wasn't prepared for the one huge fur store with its wonderful, life-size exhibition of Eskimos. It was as good as a museum.

A large apartment building stood next to and towered over one of the log cabins I had imagined. It was a sweet little cabin almost lost amongst the blue delphiniums, which grew around it, and there was a tiny window on the front overlooking the street. Perhaps it had once overlooked nothing but snow. The streets were unpaved and the sidewalks were wooden. Walking on them made a nice sound. An Eskimo mother with her baby slung in her parka hood was walking next to and chatting with a lady who would have looked at home on New York's Fifth Avenue. The noise and confusion depressed me and the dust from those unpaved streets was awful. It seemed to me that everyone was rushing madly to get somewhere else and so were we. We got out of Fairbanks as soon as the clothes were dry and the potatoes stashed in the grocery box.

Circle, on the Steese Highway, is our destination. Now that we are in Alaska we are seriously looking for a place to live. Somewhere along the way we discovered that homesteading is very, very expensive and so labor intensive that there is hardly time to talk to, let alone educate, eight children. We have come to the conclusion that, since Jack is a doctor, he can probably get a job most anywhere. Thus the new slant on our traveling; now we are hoping to find the perfect spot.

Maybe Circle will be it. We stopped for gas at Chatanika and discovered that the oil line was broken again. So, instead of going on to Circle, we pulled off the road beside a pretty little creek and, in the usual cold rain, we set up camp. We had a potato dinner because I hadn't been able to bring myself to pay the prices in that grocery store in Fairbanks and went to bed.

July 3

Awoke to glorious sunshine. After a large breakfast of eggs and fried potatoes we dragged everything out of the bus, shook the dust off every blanket and sleeping bag, swept and cleaned the bus. Then, in a fit of cleanliness, thanks to the proximity of the creek, washed the entire outside of the bus. Just as the last item was shaken, folded and put away, smelling all fresh and dry, the heavens opened once again and it poured. We ate our lunch in the bus and returned to Fairbanks to look for a Ford agency, again. It is Sunday but, in Alaska, everything seems to be open all the time and, sure enough, liquor stores and grocery stores were doing brisk business, so we did also. I, without a glance at prices — after all, we had to eat — loaded up on food and supplies of all kinds while Jack had fun in the liquor store. Then we purchased and installed a new oil line and were off again, this time for McKinley National Park.

As evening approached we found a peaceful spot on the Tanana River, which ran next to the road. Up went the teepee and the green tent and cook-fly on a clearing, which had probably been a construction site for the road builders. We had beautiful views of Mount Deborah and Mount Hayes, covered in pink snow, which grew pinker and darker as the twilight deepened.

We met yet another real homesteader, trapper and construction worker, who appeared out of the woods surrounding us, with two very large, snow-white dogs. The children were delighted with the dogs and we were delighted with his yarns. For hours we sat wide-eyed by the campfire while this gentleman went on and on. It was fascinating for, besides the usual bear stories, he told us

Lesh family

river stories — drownings, ice-jams, crashed skiffs and the like. At about ten o'clock, the light was dimming and a cold wind blew in off the river so we doused the fire, said good-bye to our new friends and went to bed. Dave is beginning to feel better. Thank goodness. He hasn't had much fun in the past few days.

July 5

Drove down the Richardson Highway yesterday and stopped in at Paxson Lodge. It was cold and rainy again so the warmth and light in the lobby of the lodge was welcome. We don't normally go into places like this because: (a) we don't have the resources to eat out often; and (b) the whole group of us can be pretty daunting to most restaurants and motels.

"Well, I guess we could put two tables together," given out grudgingly.

"No, we can't put all of you in one room. No, we have no adjoining rooms."

"Ten orders of breakfast?"

Well, you get the idea. It all daunts me sometimes, too.

On the road again, we took the turnoff to McKinley Park, and spent the third worst night of the trip at Tangle Lakes. Pouring rain, not much room left at the campsite and a lake that was rising dangerously close to our camp. The girls, aged six and five, decided they would spend the night "way up there, Dad, on the hill." So Jack went with them up to the top of the hill and, to every camper's amazement, proceeded to set up the little pup tent for these two brave little girls. They stood outside their tent in their nighties and waved cheerily to me, then crawled in and slept soundly all night, while the rest of us worried about rising water and high winds, both of which were happening. And, for the second time, the tent tried to blow over.

*   *   *   *   *

This morning the girls came down, all dressed and carrying their sleeping bags, ready for breakfast, which was one more dismal meal in the rain. This was also one more spot where I was too afraid to ride in the bus so I walked out to the road where Jack met me. Jim and Dave came along to keep me company. As we sloshed along in our raingear, I wondered for the hundredth time if we really did want to move to Alaska.

July 6

This morning we met the Gracious family. They lived in and operated a sort of roadhouse, lodge, campground and summer home. We drove the dirt road leading to Mount McKinley Park and came upon the Gracious House about mid-morning and stopped for coffee. Mrs. Gracious was all of that, and more. She said we could camp on their property and then she said I could use her oven if I had a mind to. I did have a mind to, and set to work. I baked six loaves of bread and four loaves of raisin cake, which Jack's mother used to call Poverty Cake and which we all loved. What wonderful treats: fresh bread and fresh cakes! We ate almost three loaves of the bread for lunch — for once there was butter and always there was that sixteen-pound pail of peanut butter, now down to about five pounds.

Here we learned about permafrost for the first time. We'd read about it and assumed it only occurred way up north, but after all, we were way up north and here it was. Mr. Gracious was digging a new pit for his outhouse. It wouldn't be needed for four or five more years but there was the permafrost. He dug down through the dirt that had turned into mud and then he was stopped a foot or two down by ice. By the end of the summer he would be able to dig another foot or so and then would be compelled to wait until the following summer to go the next few feet. Patience is a Required Course in Alaska.

Having washed clothes at the Gracious House and fortified ourselves with a last cup of hot coffee in that warm, friendly cafe, we were on the road again heading for the park. The country is barren but beautiful, open rolling hills covered with large mats of tiny colorful flowers. Got to McKinley in time to see a demonstration of sled dogs pulling sleds — over sand!

We got mail here: letters from home and developed photographs. I must remember to take more pictures of the kids and less of scenery. One letter we got from LIFE magazine was sort of disappointing. They have decided not to do a feature article on us because our trip story is too much like the saga of the Fifty-Niners, a group of people from Detroit who had gone to Alaska in 1959 in order to "get away from it all." The magazine did their story last year. I recalled that story and remember having been struck by the final, poignant picture taken of what was left of the group. There were four enormous logs laid up for the first "round" of a cabin. The owner and builder was standing with his axe on one of the logs and a light snow was falling. Another dream biting the dust. In one way I am relieved that there will be no more photographers and reporters but, in another way, I am sorry that all our friends back home won't see that we have made it and lived to tell the tale.

July 7

Mount McKinley National Park and, with our luck in weather, it is cold and rainy. What else? We made our camp last night close to the entrance to the park, near the lodge, because we wanted to see the nature movies and to go on a nature walk in the hopes of learning the names of the gorgeous wildflowers blooming so profusely all over this area. The movies were not only wonderful, but we were all warm and dry. In fact we were so warm and dry that all the children became flushed and uncomfortable. They probably like cold rain by now. I do not and never will.

The nature walk did give us names for the flowers: chiming bells are tall blue flowers, which grow along the roadside; small lavender asters; bright yellow arnica; delicate down-hanging bells, called twinflowers because two are borne on a stalk; purple spires of monk's hood; shrubby cinquefoil, which has a lovely yellow blossom; wild geranium, a fragile light purple; and, of course, fireweed, which is everywhere — also dwarf fireweed, which is even more lovely. The girls were dying to pick bunches and bunches for bouquets but park rules forbade it. "But Mummy! There's millions!"

*   *   *   *   *

Still cold and rainy. I gather that this is normal weather for Mount McKinley; the mountain is shy and wants to stay hidden. So I repaired to the hotel and there, in the nice warm lobby, peopled with warm, dry adults, I had a big bowl of mushroom soup and spent the rest of the afternoon writing my article for the newspaper back home and shopping for gifts for family and friends. I bought ivory crochet hooks made by Eskimos for my sister-in-law Lois, Grandma and myself; a bracelet for Mother — all different colored stones and very pretty; key rings made from the teeth of walrus, which had been buried for who knows how long and had taken on the color of the earth where they had lain, for the men of the family; Apache tear earrings for Jack's sister Ruth because they looked like her; and postcards galore. I looked for something for my sister Ree's new baby; but didn't find anything, and think maybe I'll knit something. After all this luxurious warmth I mailed my article and some letters and went back, in the usual cold drizzle, to camp, where I found Jim and Dave starting off with packs for Mount Healy. They climbed up, had supper and came back down about bedtime.

Jack cooked dinner; I saw him crouching there by the fire when I came back from the lodge. He served up macaroni and cheese, canned mustard greens, which were surprisingly good, salad, then finished with canned peaches, everyone's favorite.

After supper we went to yet another nature movie at the lodge. Walking back to camp we talked the kids into getting ready for bed while we went for a walk. Maybe they were as tired of us as we were of them because they agreed. Off we went to the beaver dam to watch those interesting animals for a while. I loved the sound they made when they flapped their tails on the water, as a danger signal, I thought. The evening light was watery and sunny at the same time — made everything dreamy and golden.

*   *   *   *   *

Years later: The following is from a series of articles I wrote for the Cape Cod Standard-Times.

Vast Alaska Described By Falmouth Traveler

By MRS. JACK K. LESH

ALASKA, Early August — A few words about Alaska.

It's enormous. It's wonderful. It's exciting!

When I tell you that all of Switzerland could fit inside of McKinley National Park and that the park is only a very small part of the whole state, you may get the idea of Alaska's size.

Or when I tell you that you can climb to the top of almost any mountain and look in all directions and as far as you can see there are no roads and no people — just wilderness — maybe you can grasp its vastness. Outdoors it is a wild, beautiful, clear cleanness and inside a log cabin it is a snug, coffee-smelling warmness.

Inside and outside you feel the freedom of the North.

The Alaskan Highway is a dusty ribbon of road, flung across the wilderness, and civilization ends just a few feet off the road. And even that civilization is spaced far apart. Sometimes you'll drive for thirty or forty miles and then come upon a gas pump outside a log cabin. Sometimes you can buy a cup of coffee and a doughnut. Usually the gas stations are unannounced. Once in a while there will be a small sign, homemade of course, and sometimes even misspelled, propped up with rocks alongside the road.

Nothing is finished up here. The roofs still have a few long ends which never get cut off. The mailbox is just stuck out on the end of a long pole which is "just temporary of course," but you know it will be like that 'till it falls down.

The oil drum, Alaska's national flower or blot on the landscape, is always but always just rolled to one side "until." There are empty oil drums all over Alaska, in every yard, on every abandoned construction site and in every vacant lot.

Some people paint them and try to make them look like something else, but they still look awful. There are always piles of things lying around people's yards. Alaskans are great savers and never throw anything away, only their houses have no attics so they save things outside the house.

Besides lumber and oil drums, the next favorite thing to save is antlers. Every house is decorated with at least one set of antlers and one enterprising man made an antler tree to stand in his front yard.

It was lovely … if you like antlers.

And everyone up here has a "green thumb" or the soil is especially good. Whatever it may be, the flowers around the dooryards are simply gorgeous — often the delphinium grows higher than the log cabin roofs and the colors are rich and beautiful. Even the lowly petunia is luxuriant and truly striking.

The lack of billboards and signs is a blessing.

There simply are none and everyone is glad of it. While driving along looking at the wonderful scenery nobody, but nobody, wants a glaring, usually unattractive picture of a man sweating and drinking beer. Or anything else for that matter. There may be a small sign simply saying "gas-food 1 mile, Dot and Mac" or one we saw which announced "English River – 3 Miles." And a few miles further another sign, reading, "Looking for English River? Here it is."

Very refreshing.

And, as I stated before, all of the signs are homemade, which makes them all the more interesting. Some are even made with pencil or cardboard — "just temporary, of course."

Alaskans are nice.

They love to talk and will stop almost anything to talk about their hunting or fishing exploits. There is no "Alaskan accent." The country is so new and so recently settled that the people still talk the way they did "back in the lower forty-eight."

You hear a lot of southern accents up here — probably Air Force and now and then you may catch a broad "A" of Boston. I love it. I haven't been here long enough to have heard any Alaskan sayings except that you are either "inside" or "outside" Alaska, or "going in" or "coming out."

One night we went to a community fish fry. The salmon run was on so the fish was fried salmon steak and was accompanied by the usual potluck covered dishes — and some unusual ones. I had moose casserole which was delicious and reindeer steaks which were ditto.

And naturally green jello — or as my children call it "lime slime." Will there ever be a church supper without it? Please invite me if there is.

But at this supper we met a lot of homesteaders. I don't know why I had expected them to look poor and disillusioned, but I did. They were neither. That group of people was absolutely indistinguishable from any other group of Americans at a community supper anywhere.

Some gals wore housedresses, some wore jeans, some wore perfectly beautiful English tweeds and some wore lovely dinner dresses. The men wore either overalls, or coat and tie or sports clothes. And the children were all healthy and rosy and dressed like the boys and girls at home.

So I feel better about homesteaders. I know they work terribly hard to carve their homes out of the wilderness, but they are doing it with real class.

July 8

Time to move on so we packed up and drove to the end of the park road, ninety miles away. The usual torpor was just settling in when Mike, who was driving, suddenly stopped so we could all see our first grizzly. He was quite far away, thank goodness, but we could easily see his hump, and we watched him for a while through the binoculars. Next we saw a whole flock of mountain sheep grazing on a hillside; then two foxes, with dinner in their mouths, crossed the road in front of us and; lastly, a grazing caribou in the distance. It was everything we hoped for and it was a tired but enthusiastic bunch of Leshes that climbed out of the bus at Wonder Lake campground. We had the place to ourselves so we chose the best campsite and settled in for a stay of several days. It is glorious, utterly beautiful and absolutely quiet. Maybe I'll stay after all.

July 9

This morning it had started to clear. I made the usual break-fast of twelve-grain cereal with brown sugar and four-in-one cream and listened to the usual grumbles. Some day I'll shock them all and give them bacon and eggs. They managed to choke it down along with buttered toast, made on the top of the camp stove and hot sweet cocoa. After camp chores it was free time for everyone so they all vanished. The boys, with the exception of Mike, went off exploring. One boy stayed in camp to watch the little children while Jack, Mike and I hiked over the tundra to the ranger station, seeking permission to put the canoe in Wonder Lake. The park has a nice rule: No motors of any kind are allowed on the lake. You can almost hear the silence — you can certainly hear people talking a long way off. On the way back we passed a very small pond with one tiny baby duck swimming frantically in circles, grabbing mosquitoes out of the air with his baby beak — trying desperately to grow up so he could leave this pond and find some friends. I'll remember that small, determined scrap of yellow fluff for a long time.

Since the sun was out I set the boys to carrying water for me so I could wash the ever-present pile of dirty clothes. I stripped everything off Tom and Bets and let them run around all bare while their clothes were washed and dried. The bushes were loaded with drying clothes but it didn't take long for them to dry in the hot sun. I gave Sally Ann and Bets and Tom baths in the washtub, too; small bare people, drying in the sun as they ran around and played in the dirt again. No caretakers here. By supper, everyone was dressed and clean

Then it happened! The Mountain, as it is called hereabouts, came into view! The clouds pulled away from each side, like cur-tains at a play, and there it was, in all its glory and might. Even the children were awed. I could hear them whispering to each other during the night as, one by one, they woke up to look at that huge pile of snow and rock in the brilliant moonlight.

Lesh family

July 10

Jack's birthday and his only gift is the fact that we are as far north and west as the roads go — nothing beyond here but ancient world, no roads or cities or people.

At 4:30 a.m. we were awakened by a newly arrived camper who was so thrilled by the sight of the mountain, that he went around waking everybody — even Tom and Bets and Sally Ann in their little pup tent. That wonderful mountain was an awesome sight, pale rose, lavender and dazzling white. So enthralled was everyone that further sleep was impossible and the entire camp stayed up for the glory of it.

Jim was the first to spot a moose. He'd been sitting around the camp trying to entice some little ground squirrels to come and eat out of his hand when he heard something walking in the weeds and snorting now and then. Looking up, he beheld antlers moving just above the top of the low shrubs. They were moving slowly, bobbing up and down as the animal fed but coming closer and closer to Jim. He stood his ground bravely until the antlers were almost upon him, then, giving way to panic, he stood up to run. At that precise moment Pete and Jon, who were carrying the antlers, burst into loud guffaws. While they fell on the ground in helpless giggles, poor Jim, bellowing with rage and frustration, ran off to tell. Fat lot of good it did him to tell — all we could do was laugh.

The gentleman who had awakened us to see the mountain came around often and once when we were eating lunch, there he was again; so we invited him to join us. One of our lunchtime favorites is a very thin, almost paper-thin, Swedish flat bread. He seemed rather fascinated by the stuff and started to eat it. After chewing thoughtfully for some time he said, "A man could starve to death while eating this stuff."

> **Years later:** The boys latched on to this statement right away and at almost every lunch thereafter one of them was sure to say, "Gosh! A man could starve to death while eating this stuff."

For a change of scenery we took a picnic and drove to Moose Creek, close by the Kantishna Mining Camp. This camp consisted of a group of several small, weather-beaten cabins, mostly deserted but for one, which had smoke coming out of its rickety chimney. We knocked on the door and a smiling woman invited us all in and spent an hour or so showing us her gold nuggets, some of which were huge.

The interior of the cabin was gray and dusty. Boxes and boxes full of rocks and stones stood everywhere, their gray color blending in with all the rest. The only spot of color in the whole building was a bunch of purple lupine that had been thrust into a canning jar and now graced the table full of boxes of rocks. The woodstove, an ancient, rusty black monster in the corner was hot and we could smell something delicious. "Oh, excuse me," she said suddenly and went to the stove. Opening the rusty door of the oven, she removed no less than three lemon meringue pies! It's all I could do to manage one in my well-equipped kitchen back home, but here was this indomitable woman, with an old wood-stove, taking three pies out. We were stunned. And even more stunned when she offered us one of them! She told us we should go to Friday Creek nearby and pan for gold, so we did. We got the gold pans out of the bus and went to work in the icy waters of the tumbling creek and before long, the boys had several tiny nuggets and flakes of gold. Once again they were all convinced that we could become rich by panning for gold, until we showed them approximately the amount that made up an ounce, and told them that the going rate was thirty-five dollars an ounce. A little quick arithmetic and a short lecture on economics from Jack soon took care of that pipe dream. So instead of hoarding it all for a rainy day, they gallantly gave it all to their dad for a birthday gift.

Back to camp to make a late supper. Jon decided to make a cake for Jack and did so, putting the batter into a pan and the pan into the little folding oven, which he set on the gas stove in the bus — a very precarious arrangement. Unfortunately Jack, knowing nothing of Jon's plan, decided to move the bus. The pan slid to one side and came to rest at an angle. Large globs of yellow batter ran down the sides of the oven and dripped onto the floor before anyone noticed. After the oven was righted the batter continued to bake in a desultory manner resulting in a cake that was not only lopsided, but also burned on one side and soupy on the other. Jack was game and so were the rest of us and we ate every crumb.

July 11

We were up at 4:00 a.m. to get an early start in order to have a better chance of seeing wild animals. Not one animal was out this morning. When we arrived once again at the campsite near the McKinley Hotel, we stopped and cooked up a huge breakfast

— bacon and eggs and fried potatoes. Wowed them. Thence to Tangle Lakes again, where the weather is better and the water in the lake is lower. And, as we arrived early, we got the best campsite. But still no fish.

July 12

Drove to a campsite outside of Palmer. As we drove along through this mostly open country, we were startled to come upon a sign by the side of the road advertising Checker Cabs for Sale Just Ahead. Checker Cabs? The last one of those I'd seen was in New York City — what on earth would a person want with a taxi cab in this practically total wilderness? Well, we drove a bit more when, sure enough, there was a brightly painted Checker Cab complete with a for-sale sign parked on a small hill in front of a barn. And, while we were in the area, we heard of a farmer who made some kind of intoxicating drink out of cow's milk. And I thought I'd heard everything.

July 13

Drove around Palmer looking for Jim's pen pal. During their Alaska studies at school, the children had been persuaded to write to kids in Alaska and somehow Jim got the name of Debbie Demming. Her dad owned and operated a roadhouse in Big Butte, a sort of suburb of Palmer. There was a butte there too, a very large butte, such as might be seen in the Southwest United States, a great huge rock rising up out of otherwise flat ground. We found the roadhouse and suddenly Jim, who had been so anxious to get there, was nowhere to be seen. He was hiding back by the grocery bin. After a bit of urging from Jack, "Damn it, you wanted to come here, now here we are." Jim pulled himself together and managed to walk up to the front door. Nobody was home. A neighbor came over and told us the entire Demming family had gone to New York for the summer. Hard to tell if Jim was relieved or disappointed.

So we drove on to Anchorage, arriving there before noon and, to save time, ate a quick lunch in the bus. We'd parked in a public parking lot and were eating when a large, happy man came over to the bus to welcome us to Alaska. His name was Col. Marston and he told us that he'd "done a lot with the Eskimos." What it was that he did we didn't find out. But, as he told us, it was a lot. He'd been with the Army National Guard in the Far North of Alaska. When he discovered what we were doing in Alaska, he wanted us to go north, beyond the road system, and raise potatoes. We thanked him for his thoughtfulness, but we had already decided on a plan for our immediate futures.

A second gentleman appeared at the bus door shortly thereafter and announced that his name too was Lesh, and that he owned a Piggly-Wiggly store there in Anchorage. He sported a wristwatch with gold nuggets at least a half an inch thick set into the band. It was a gorgeous, flashy hunk of gold and we truly felt we were in the presence of a real Alaskan at last. He was a bit abashed at seeing so many eager Lesh faces and I think was glad to say good-bye. We had heard about Mr. Lesh earlier, especially that he was very wealthy. Perhaps, as he surveyed our gang in torn jeans and none-too-clean shirts, he was afraid a large bunch of indigent relatives was going to hit him up for a loan. He was very pleasant, but it was evident he was in a hurry to leave.

The tourist center in Anchorage was housed in a small log cabin in the middle of town. A perfectly delightful lady, Natalie Hewlett, ran the place and was most helpful, telling us all the places where we could camp, and where to shop and so on. As we stood there chatting away, a Muriel Hannah came in to hang a picture. Subsequent conversation revealed that this very morning she had gotten a letter from a friend back East in Falmouth, Massachusetts, who had written Mrs. Hannah, "to be sure to be on the lookout for a large yellow school bus, with her friends, the

Leshes, on board." She didn't even have to look out for us — we just bumped into each other.

Lesh family

The boys took their "best-ests" and went off to explore the city while I did the usual shopping and laundry. I took time to buy some presents for the upcoming birthdays, also.

We took off for a campground Natalie Hewlett had told us about, twenty-five miles south of Anchorage, on Turnagain Arm. It is a wonderful spot. A small point juts out into the water of Turnagain Arm with huge trees, outhouses and only three camp-sites. We have it to ourselves and have settled in for a day or two.

July 14

We were planning to leave the children at the campground while we went back to Anchorage to have the bus fixed: kingpins this time. We gave a long lecture to the children, full of dire warnings about the mudflats, which stretched out invitingly in front of the campground. We'd heard about the bore tide that races down the inlet at every high tide and were terrified lest one or all of the children would be caught in it, so we really laid down the law and the rules for the day. Then Jack and I were off in the bus. While the kingpins, whatever they do, were being taken care of at the garage, Jack and I toured the town with Natalie in her car. We had a lovely lunch with her and I did more shopping. Natalie told us that a Dr. Fritz would be driving down to the camp tonight to visit us. He was an eye, ear, nose and throat doc-tor and flew all over Alaska seeing patients. With that to look for-ward to, we drove on back to the campsite hoping for a quiet afternoon with the children.

When we pulled in at the camp, we could see things were not as they should be. There were new campers: a man in shiny clothes, his wife in white skirt and blouse and their equally clean little boy, who was about ten years old. The parents were very, very upset with us because we had left the children alone. Alone? Each older boy had his own special charge of one of the younger children and would take good care to keep them off the mudflats, while they themselves didn't dare venture out on the mud for fear another brother would tattle. So we knew they were all right. But there was more. When the new family of campers had arrived they had asked how many children were there, out all alone, and had been told there were eight. But they could only count seven. Who was missing? Nobody knew. Everyone knew where everyone else was, and the campgrounds were limited on all sides by mud flats. Well, why are there only seven here?

This went on for some time, and suddenly Sally Ann spoke up, "I guess you mean Tom. We're playing house and he's the dog so we tied him up in Mom's tent and he went to sleep."

The poor distraught mother of one threw up her hands and disappeared into their trailer.

Dr. Fritz and his wife Betsy did come, bringing ice cream and watermelon, which the children shared with the clean little boy, whose mother washed his face immediately after he was through eating, and we all sat around the campfire drinking coffee. The Fritzes told us they had a cabin at Anchor Point and that we could use it for as long as a week if we wanted to. Then Mrs. Fritz suggested that I come to her house to do laundry the next day and, of course, I told her I would be delighted. "Bring the children," this good woman said, so we planned on it.

July 15

At the Fritzes' house, when lunchtime arrived there were hamburgers for all, so we sat down to eat.

Just as I was taking the first bite, Dr. Fritz suddenly leapt from his chair. "Whoops!" he cried, dashed into the laundry room and shut off the washing machine. I was a bit startled to say the least, wondering what I had done to annoy him. Maybe broken the washer?

"No machines at mealtime," he said and sat down to his lunch.

The kids could hardly keep from laughing so they stuffed their mouths with hamburger and didn't dare look at one another.

> **Years later:** For the rest of the trip and for some years later, it was "no machines at mealtime," and off they would go into gales of hilarity.

Eager to keep up with that mother back at the camp, I bathed the three youngest and combed everyone's hair and we were back in camp by mid-afternoon. The clean family, disturbed no doubt by the proximity of noisy and neglected children, had left and we had a quiet evening, exploring the woods on the other side of the road and looking for berries.

July 16

We left the Turnagain Arm campground this morning fairly early. Jim and Dave had finished their chores and wanted to start walking down the road toward Kenai. As there is only the one road, they couldn't get lost or take a wrong turn. We agreed to their request, and would pick them up on the way. They had walked quite a way along the highway when suddenly a large-sounding rig pulled up behind them and almost came to a stop. It was that same couple, the clean ones, who had gone back to Anchorage the night before and were also on their way to the Kenai, when who should they run into but two of those poor, abandoned children. Jim and Dave waved cheerily to their shocked faces and watched them roll out of sight, the little boy looking wistfully out of the back window.

*   *   *   *   *

Today we started our search for J.T., the fellow whose baby Jack had taken care of a while back on the road. He was the one who offered his cabin to us in case we needed a place to live. We drove to the Miller Loop Road, where he had said his place was and looked all over for him. Nobody had ever heard of him. Nobody knew of a J.T. and nobody knew of any cabin, now locked up, by a pond where his logs floated. He had also asked us to turn his logs in the pond, so they would season evenly on all sides.

"No, there was no cabin up that road."

"J.T.? No, never heard the name."

"Who? No."

During the search we did meet some very nice people. One lady, who keeps Saanen goats, showed us all around her barn and homestead. We had kept goats back in Falmouth because Mike was very allergic to cow's milk. We had all learned to like it, or at least tolerate the stuff. It was nice to know that goats can thrive in this climate. But we never found a trace of J.T. Come to think of it, logs don't need to be turned; they float one way only. What a great storyteller that man was, or are we more gullible than most?

We left Kenai and headed south in search of Dr. Fritz's cabin. And we wondered if that too was a hoax. It wasn't. We found it, in Anchor Point, and parked the bus in the neighbor's back yard. That neighbor, Mrs. Mutsh, invited us all to come to a community fish fry that night, so we washed up and joined the crowd.

The food, spread out on two picnic tables, was too good to be true: pink salmon steaks sizzled over a charcoal fire watched over by a gentleman whose nose was the same color as the salmon; deep-fried bits of king crab leg; huge, bubbling pots of baked beans; loaves of home-baked bread cut into thick slices; four or five salads made up of fresh green lettuces; casseroles galore; and a staggering array of cakes and pies — apple pies, blueberry pies, raisin pies, chocolate pies and even a pecan pie! The drinks were wonderful also: wild cranberry juice, lemonade, strong coffee and a couple of cases of beer. The kids were in heaven and tasted everything in sight. The people were friendly and welcoming. The children, healthy, sturdy and strong, seemed to be smiling all the time. I was enchanted with all of it.

Dr. Fritz's two-story log cabin sits on a high bluff overlooking Cook Inlet. We are so ready for a vacation from the bus that we moved everything inside and prepared to stay for a few days. Tom and the two girls climbed the ladder leading to the loft and put their sleeping bags on the floor. Jack and I took the bed downstairs: A real bed. The boys put up the teepee quite far from us — cabin fever setting in, or bus fever — and we all look forward to our stay. It is fun to cook on a real stove again, albeit a woodstove, so we had a grand dinner and played games in the warm, dry room before going to bed.

July 17

We spent the day loafing around the cabin. I baked bread and a raisin pie. Before Atlin I had never had raisin pie nor had the rest of the family, but now we all love it; Greenjeans Pie we call it. The ingredients are so easy to store, too. Just packages of raisins; one hopes to have the flour, sugar and lard on hand also. The day was clear and quite warm and the kids swarmed over the place, exploring and whooping and yelling — sheer joy at being free from the confines of the bus or the rules in parks.

July 18

We left the poor, neglected kids at the cabin, and Jack and I drove to Homer to have a look at the town. What a beautiful spot! High, rolling meadows, sparse timber and a spectacular view out over Katchemak Bay and the Homer Spit. The spit isn't much wider than the road and runs a long, long way out into the bay — just sand and wisps of grass. There is a forest on the spit. About five wind-beaten trees grow on one little spot, all huddled together, leaning away from the wind in order to survive. But it is a forest. It may even be called a national forest.

Homer, to me, was Vermont, Cape Cod and Atlin all rolled into one! I loved it and was ready to go house hunting. We soon found that the resident doctor was not overworked and that land prices were extremely high. Our friend Natalie Hewlett from the Anchorage Visitor's Center had lived in Homer for a long time.

Her husband had owned a bank here and when he died she had learned to run it herself until it could be sold. She has such fond memories of the place that she has infected us with that enthusiasm. And I, for one, am tired of traveling.

We ate fried king crab on the sunny beach and wallowed in the smells and sounds of salt water. A man rowed into the dock with a one-hundred-pound halibut in his boat. What a sight! The skiff was pretty well bashed up from the thrashing halibut tail and was full of water. The fisherman was still smiling though, as hands reached down to help him unload. It was all very exciting and we should have brought the kids.

July 19

Returned to Homer with the children, but, wouldn't you know, the cannery was closed. So we spent most of the afternoon talking with a resident who showed us all the wonderful things she was growing in her garden. And we talked with lots of other folks, asking about living here and how to homestead and what about schools, etc. We listened to tales of woe and tales of good luck from both homesteaders and business people. It was disturbing to learn that homesteading can be more expensive than just buying a ready-made house with cleared land under it.

July 21

Yesterday we left the children, yet again, and drove to Ninilchik, a lovely, small fishing village built on the beach at the mouth of the Ninilchik River where it empties into Cook Inlet. Over time, the river had eroded a deep valley so we left the highway and crept down the steep road leading into the village. The little gray wood houses were close to each other and close to the dirt road, the main and only street. Behind them, rising practically straight up from the back doors, the hill began. We walked up the little stony path that led to the top of the hill. On the top there was a dear little Russian Orthodox church, white-painted with a white picket fence surrounding the tiny green lawn in front. The onion-shaped dome on top was painted gold and the whole thing couldn't have taken up more than twenty feet or so, either way. Apparently a priest came once in a while to conduct services, for there was a hand-penciled note to that effect, tacked to the door. The next service would be in November.

We walked back down the path a bit to where another smaller, stonier path led off towards the edge of the bluff and the lighthouse. It was the smallest lighthouse in the world, I think. It was merely a kerosene lantern hanging on the end of a long, skinny board nailed to a solid post, both painted white and obviously lovingly cared for. The lantern burns all the time, day and night, year round, and is kept burning by a dedicated soul who thinks the fishermen, returning late at night, need it. And need it they must, for the shore along here is one long, unbroken bluff. It would be only too easy to miss the entrance to the river, especially in the dark.

The charred skeleton of the old school was on this hill, too. What a marvelous place to go to school, on top of the world with views to the end of it in every direction out its windows; perfectly grand for daydreaming young minds. It too was painted white and it might have held as many as fifteen children in one room. There were two little, white-painted outhouses in the back yard and absolutely no playground equipment. The whole universe was right outside that little door. What need had the children for anything else?

Now they go up to the highway to a new school with windows overlooking the traffic, and there are probably swings and teeter-totters, too. I adored Ninilchik but apparently nobody else did, for many of the houses were empty. Maybe the fish are gone.

When we got back to the cabin we found three of the boys embroiled in some sort of a fracas. I think fists had been used, for they were, all three of them, unusually subdued, unusually rumpled, as well as unusually bruised. Mike and the younger children had left in disgust and were at the beach finding glass balls, which had been washed up on shore, and clumps of coal for the stove.

During the night, one of the children, sleeping in the loft overhead, threw up all over the floor. Since this is just a cabin, there were cracks in that floor, wide cracks, down through which the stuff dripped. Quite a clean-up job was required and, of course, there was no hot water. It was one of those times, all too frequent now, that I wondered what we were getting into. More and more I am leaning toward plumbing and a furnace.

*   *   *   *   *

Drove back to Homer Spit today to take the kids to the cannery, but it was closed again. Instead, while everyone else explored, I washed the dirty clothes in a small town Alaska version of a laundromat. There were three "stations," for lack of a better word, each consisting of one wringer-washer surrounded by three washtubs. There was hot water so I went to work. You put a load of wash into the wringer tub, add hot water and soap and let the machine run until you think the clothes are clean, then stop the machine. Next you wring them into a waiting washtub full of rinse water. Then you swing the wringer arm around and wring the clothes into a second tub of rinse water, and from there you wring them into the final, empty tub and you're done … except for the next load, which has by now been started in the machine and is ready to go through the wringer and rinse processes. It really worked very well and when I was done I took the clean, wet clothes out to the bus to hang up on Dr. Fritz's clothesline.

For supper we bought two enormous king crabs, and back to the cabin we went to feast on french-fried crab. Batter for french-fried crab: two cups of flour, one egg and enough flat beer to make pancake-batter consistency. Delicious. I hate to leave the relative comfort of the Fritzes' cabin, but it is time to move along. Summer is half over and we have lots of miles to go and lots of decisions to make.

July 22

Left the haven of Dr. Fritz's cabin and headed north to Kenai Lake where we spent the night at Quartz Creek campground. There is a small combination grocery store-cafe-gas station nearby and we spent a couple of hours talking to the couple that owned and ran it. They told us all about the environs; stories of moose abounded. This spot is beautiful but there are not enough people here to support an MD with eight children. And the saltwater is too far away. Supper was a so-so meal: canned corned-beef hash, fried potatoes and canned peas. We trooped over to the cafe for ice cream and coffee afterwards; listened to more bear and moose tales; then went back to the camp; and, after the bedtime story for the littlest ones, we went to bed.

July 23

Jim's birthday. From Kenai Lake we drove back to Anchorage to do some shopping and get mail. Mail pickups are always fun. Fun to hear from family and friends about their doings. I got a little teary when I read of all the family gatherings and, for a moment or two, would have liked to be back home. But we are not going. We are finally in Alaska, where we have been planning to be for two years now, so I'd better buck up and enjoy it. Off to Willow and its surrounding country.

*   *   *   *   *

We pulled into a campground there in Willow, only to find it so crowded with people and tents and cars that we drove right out again and headed for Palmer, via the road to Little Susitna Lodge and Hatcher Pass.

Jim had started to get pains in his stomach and, by the time we stopped, he didn't want his birthday dinner. We had bought fresh vegetables at a roadside stand — green beans, tomatoes and lettuce — to go with the hamburgers he had desired. Dave was going to make a cake for him but Jim was so sick and the hour was so late that we cancelled the cake. I gave Jim his presents and he cheered up a little but it was a dreary birthday for him. To make camp we just drove off to the side of the road to a small clearing next to a pretty little pond where ducks and geese floated serenely. Peaceful and beautiful. Happy birthday, Jim.

Lesh family

July 24

It was a long, long drive up extremely steep hills to get over Hatcher Pass today, but supremely beautiful. The road was narrow and dirt and, of course, a light rain was falling. By lunch we had reached Little Susitna Lodge, which was for sale as the manager told us when we went in for coffee. The kids ate in the bus while we visited with this functionary and, by the time we were ready to leave, I was ready to buy the place and run it as a ski lodge. As Jack dragged me out I was planning the decor and my wardrobe. What fun it would have been. And what a huge amount of work. Instead we drove to Eagle River campground and made camp in the rain. It wasn't cold, just drippy, as we sat around the stove under the tarp eating our supper of Dinty Moore beef stew and biscuits, when the neighboring camper strolled over to say hello.

We had observed him and his family of small children. He had stretched a huge sheet of Visqueen over their entire camp and the children went around poking at the plastic with sticks, making the huge puddles that had formed on it pour down like water out of a pitcher. The kids were having a great time as the water ran down their fronts but I could see their mother wasn't having much fun at all. She was in the Crouch over a smoking fire and muttering to herself as she stirred something that smelled burned. The father, who had wandered over to our camp, one Mr. Stokes, was from Juneau.

"I see you're from Massachusetts," he said. "So am I. Where do you live?"

We told him we were looking for a place to live where there was a possibility for Jack to practice medicine and that we had not planned to return to Massachusetts. But opportunities were not appearing in any great numbers, so we were beginning to have second thoughts about the entire venture.

"Oh. You're a doctor?" he asked.

"Yes," replied Jack, "but it looks as though there's no room for another one."

Mr. Stokes stroked his beard and offered, "Well, in the past year down in Juneau, two doctors have dropped dead of heart attacks and maybe …."

He got no further: "That's why we left the Cape, too many doctors dropping dead of heart attacks," I announced. "That's why we came to Alaska, to lead a more sensible kind of life. No cities, either," I concluded irrationally.

Mr. Stokes, baffled by my outburst, said in a conciliatory way, "Well, I just wondered, you know. Recently I've been writing to various MDs around the country and here in Alaska to see if any of them might be interested in coming to Juneau to practice. I'll be around here for a couple more days and we can talk some more." And he went back to his camp under the plastic sheeting.

Of course we did talk about it, at great length, too. I hate rain and it rains all the time in Juneau but so far we haven't seen any real need for physicians in the small towns we have visited.

This evening two enormous truck-vans drove into the camp. There were seventy-two giggling women of all ages on board the vans; it was the Alberta Recreational Society touring Alaska and they are spending the night in this camp, right next to us. The children are fascinated and we all wonder why there aren't any men in the group. Don't they get to travel for recreation, too? The girls whooped and hollered and sang and ran around laughing for half the night. They too must be suffering from bus fever!

July 25

Got up in the rain. The Stokes family had left their camp and gone to Anchorage for the day, leaving buckets under the biggest drips, and a perfectly miserable little dog tied to a tent pole. We also left for Anchorage to do some shopping. We parked the bus downtown, headed for the nearest grocery store, and there we ran into Vince Doran. We had met Vince back in Falmouth and he had told us at that time to be sure to look him up, but we had lost his address and had forgotten all about him. He had seen the bus parked outside and followed us into the store. We had coffee and chatted while Jack telephoned Dr. Whitehead, one of the physicians Stokes had suggested we call. In the telephone conversation he'd told Jack to come on down to Juneau and "we can talk."

"He spoke with a deep Southern accent," reported Jack. I said I wouldn't mind being left in the camp for a few days if he really wanted to go and see about a possible job.

When Vince, to his everlasting credit, said, "Sally, you and the kids could live in my house for a week while Jack goes to Juneau. My wife and kids are outside for the summer and I'll be leaving soon, too."

He didn't have to ask me twice; I was in there with the kids in no time flat, while Jack and the boys went back to the camp to get the tents and so on. All three little ones were soon in the tub with a half-foot of bubble-bath suds and I was in the kitchen baking a hamburger pie for dinner. All that camping fun was forgotten in the delights of a stove you worked with buttons and warmth you got from a radiator and not a fire pit — not to mention refrigeration. I don't care how long Jack will be gone. Vince isn't leaving until tomorrow but still there is room for all of us to sleep in the house! What luxury.

July 26

Vince drove Jack to the airport at 7:00 a.m. The boys took the kids downtown to a playground so I had the house to myself for the whole day. It was sheer bliss. I baked, washed, read a magazine while my hair dried, and enjoyed every second of the peace which passeth understanding, unless you are a mother. The kids came back about 6:00 p.m., in time for supper and a long summer evening in a real yard by a real house in a real town. What was all that about wilderness living?

July 27

Same program as yesterday except I CLEANED THE BUS! It was shiny inside and out, no dust or mud anywhere. I started to put things away again in their proper places so as to be ready to go again when the time came. In the meantime, Mike fixed Vince's stove, and his radio and the toaster, none of which had been working well when we arrived

July 28

At 4:30 this afternoon we climbed into our newly clean bus and drove out to the airport, kind of expecting Jack. We sat in the airport and watched planes come in and take off until the Pacific Northwest Airlines plane from Juneau landed and Jack was on it.

He told us all about Juneau. "They have awnings over the sidewalks downtown so people don't get rained on while they are shopping. The town is built on the side of a mountain and the sidewalks are mostly stairs. Some of the streets are not paved but most are."

The doctors he'd talked with were nice. There are only two clinics in the town, no private practitioners at all. He would have to join one of the clinics and had already made up his mind which one. Yes, I would like it. Yes, there are schools. Yes, it was a bit rainy but he had been there for one beautiful sunny day and the mountains around the town and across the channel were high and panoramic. There was even snow on the tops of some. He didn't know about skiing and thought swimming might be out of the question because of frigid water, but we would see."

Well, it was either that or go back to Falmouth. By now the lure of the North has us hooked and we've decided to go on down and try it out for a year anyway. That decision made, we had a glass of wine and I cooked up a celebratory dinner of poached salmon with egg and caper sauce, and there was ice cream for dessert. We all like being in Anchorage because we can get fresh milk and cream. The Matanuska Valley is full of dairies and it is a real treat for us to be able to have fresh milk instead of that dreadful four-in-one stuff we've had here and there on the trip.

July 29

Packed up the bus, cleaned Vince's house, baked a cake and some banana bread and once more hit the road. But now the end is in sight and we all feel relieved to have made our decisions and can now look forward to a new life in a new country. There are still some days of driving and camping though, so we bought a load of groceries and headed for Haines where we will get on a ferry to go to Juneau.

Camped at Little Nelchina in pouring rain — seems every time we turn the key in the ignition the clouds roll in and the rain starts. Funny little supper under the tarp, sort of a mishmash of vegetables in the frying pan, and apples — plus the last of the real milk.

Ted Polumbaum/TimePix

July 30

Something is very wrong with the bus. Exhaust fumes are coming in somewhere and we all have headaches and the younger children are irritable and whiny. We arrived at our destination, Mirror Lake campground, too late to make a proper supper but we tried to be cheerful and, after some soup and sandwiches, we did feel better. Jack did something to the exhaust pipe and we hope tomorrow will be better. Another day like this and it's over for me; I'll take the next vehicle going in either direction.

A fellow from New Hampshire wandered over to tell us he was glad to have finally met up with us. Apparently he had been looking for us all the way. Why? Just to say hello? Must be, because after he'd said, "Hello," he wandered off again. Maybe he's related to J.T.

July 31

After drying tents and tarps that had gotten soaked during the night, we headed for Kluane Lake. The country was interesting but we have seen a lot of country and are more ready to snooze or read than look out the windows — so of course we missed the moose running across the road in front of us. Jack saw it because he was driving but the rest of us missed it. "Oh well, there'll be more," we said. And there were. Later, as we drove alongside a large pond, we could see a circle of ripples on the surface of the water. Jack stopped to see what was making those ripples when a huge moose rose right up out of the water, weeds draped all over his body and dripping out of his mouth. He had been completely underwater, eating and strolling around on the bottom. Preparing a salad, was he?

Got to Kluane Lake about 4:00 p.m. and set up our camp. The campground is very nice, spacious and clean, and has that most essential item, a shelter with a huge wood cook stove. I went to work making biscuits, which we shared with a bunch of mountain climbers. Happy Appys, they call themselves, as they are members of the Appalachian Mountain Club. They were thrilled to have hot biscuits.

Our boys had gone off to pick crowberries and I thought it would be fun to try to make jam with the berries. So I added sugar and put them on the back of the cook stove and left them there to cook gently. But I left them too long. When I tried to scoop some out of the pot with a spoon, the handle of the spoon started to bend. So I added water and got a stronger spoon. Well, it wasn't jam but it was sweet and tasted wonderful on those buttery hot biscuits.

August 2

Yesterday was Mike's birthday. We drove to Haines where we found a pretty camping spot a little way out of town and we set up the tents. Cars kept stopping to see what was going on — a teepee? And a school bus? A bus that said "Fairbanks" on the front? Since it was Mike's birthday today and Dave's birthday would be tomorrow, we decided to eat in a restaurant. The one we found was small and dark but a cheerful lady made hamburgers for all of us and, for a special treat for the birthday boys, she made banana splits — without the banana. This pleasant person also told us that there would be a special dance that night, by the Tlingit Indians for Mrs. Egan, the wife of the governor of Alaska. She was in Haines for this occasion and our informant thought it would be all right if we attended, too. She told us how to get there and off we went.

The show was being held in one of the vast old buildings built by the Army during the war, World War II that is, and still being used in various ways. The large, wooden homes that once housed officers and their families now housed just plain families. The doctor lived in one. The buildings were laid out to form a large square, originally the parade ground but now just a huge lawn, and the dance was to be performed in a dark and dusty upstairs hall. Mrs. Egan and her teenaged son Dennis were already there so we introduced ourselves and sat down to watch. The children all sat on the floor and there was nobody else there at all — we were the entire audience.

The dances, for there were several, were interesting and, during an interval between two of them, the Indians displayed a blanket, which they dedicated to Mrs. Egan. It was a most beautiful and imaginative use of fur and felt and buttons. The background was green felt but the center part was made up of small squares of fur, sewn together in such a manner as to look like patchwork, the nap of each square at right angles to the nap of the next square. The effect was stunning. Around the fur center were rows and rows of white buttons. We clapped wildly when it was all over and Mrs. Egan and I chatted together while the boys and Dennis sized each other up. It turns out that they too were going to Juneau the next day on the same ferry. As if there were any others.

And so to bed, we to our camp and the Egans to the hotel that was made up of three of those large old Army buildings. As I lay in the sleeping bag, drifting off to sleep, the night was suddenly rent with wild cries and whoops and hollers. Indians, I figured, angered by our teepee, were going to attack and scalp us. I opened the tent zipper about one inch and peered out, ready to save the little girls in the bus since Jack was peacefully snoring. Three cars of drunken young men were stopped by the camp-ground and were jeering loudly at us. Then they started blowing their horns. It was pretty noisy for a while there but they soon became tired of their game or ran out of beer, I don't know which — at last they left us with only an occasional seagull cry and the soft lapping of waves on the beach.

*   *   *   *   *

Packed up the camp and drove to the ferry landing. I was horrified to discover that the bus had to be backed onto the ferry. As if this weren't enough, the approach the drivers would back down, was a rickety affair of logs strung end to end, topped with boards just wide enough for the wheels of the vehicles. Between the two wheel paths of planking, there was nothing but water underneath. I was paralyzed with fear and wouldn't let any of the children stay on the bus while Jack backed it over those floats. Sheer madness.

But he did it and then we had to follow, also on those same log floats. Of course, in my mind the children would all slip and fall into the water and, of course, I would drown while trying to rescue them and, of course, everyone on shore would split their sides laughing and … well, none of it happened. I summoned all my courage, and with a grip that almost left bruises on their little arms, took Tom and Bets one at a time out to the ferry. Sal ran on those skinny boards all the way out while the boys just walked as if they did it every day of their lives.

Then the captain blew the whistle. We are on our way to Juneau. Mr. Stokes with his entire wet family and the wet dog, are also on board. The family had accompanied Mr. Stokes on his business trip to Anchorage so they could "get away from the rain for a while." Fat chance. It rained every day they were at the Eagle River campground with us. As we chugged down Lynn Canal, I was leaning on the rail in the drizzle, watching the icy, gray water slip away from the stern, when Mr. Stokes came to stand beside me. "The day will come," he said, "when you will think of this as a fine, fine day." I surely hope he is right, but for now I can only wonder.

August 3

Juneau: As we steamed up Gastineau Channel, there it was ahead of us, its buildings snuggled into the base of blue mountains. As we got closer we could see that the houses began at the shoreline and went right straight up the mountainsides. It looked kind of cute from the ship. As the ship was tied up, Jack said, "The crowd on the dock is all the doctors and their wives and children, as well as the entire office staff and their families, here to meet us."

Jack drove the bus, loaded with Leshes, off the ferry and onto the shore. He got out first, as was appropriate, for it was he they had hired, and I followed with all the children. Dr. Whitehead, the grand old patriarch of the clinic and a Southern gentleman to boot, was the first to step up and welcome us. He called me Miss Sally from the first moment and, of course, I was charmed with his gracious manners. We met the other doctors and all the staff; then, in the bus and two or three cars we all drove to Dr. Whitehead's cabin "out the road." Naturally, everyone wanted to ride in the bus and naturally I didn't care if I ever rode in it again so there was a great swapping around of seats and people. But we all got there and the children exploded out onto the beach in front of the Whiteheads' cabin.

Mrs. Whitehead was presiding over two large picnic tables laden with all kinds of yummy looking food and drink, so we fell to and had a grand time. At one point during the picnic I saw Dr. Whitehead watering the window boxes, which were spilling over with sweet peas and other pretty flowers. Watering? All it does is rain here, I thought, why does he have to water the flowers? I stuck my finger into the nearest flowerpot and it was bone dry. I have a lot to learn.

When the question of sleeping arrangements arose we decided to camp out for a few more nights while getting to know our way around. Dr. Whitehead led the whole procession of us to the Auke Bay Recreational Area on the way back to town. This mass of people wandered down some steps to the beach from the road and we could see a shelter, which had a huge fire pit in it. Betsy soon found the WOMEN sign. A tiny trickle of the smallest steam of water ran through the area so we were all set.

Camp was set up in no time to the astonishment of the assembled crowd, but after a bit they all drove away and we are alone on the misty beach. The water is calm and the only sounds are of gulls calling to one another. Our first night in Juneau is auspicious.

August 4

I cooked breakfast, standing up, in the shelter and we had real tables to eat from, so it was all very elegant. After the chores were done we drove into town to see the clinic and start looking for a place to live.

Mr. Stokes gallantly offered to take a couple of the boys into his home if we had to farm them out for a while. Our first stop was to deliver Jim and Dave to him, along with a whole ham as a token of our appreciation.

Juneau, Alaska

It was much later that I found out the Stokes family did not eat meat from animals with cloven hooves; I should have given them something else: a new roll of Visqueen, perhaps? One of the doctors from the clinic turned over to us his entire house, with two bedrooms, as he and his family were leaving for a vacation. Jack and I and the three little kids stayed there and Mike, Pete and Jon drove the bus out to a farm in the Mendenhall Valley and camped out in that. Now we were free to house hunt.

The clinic was downtown on South Franklin Street and the hospital was up on the hill about six blocks away. We trudged all over town looking at the very few houses for sale. They were all too small —much too small. Except one. A large, white house with green trim stood on a flat green lawn and had a nice garden out in the back yard. There were tall white pillars on the front porch, big windows to let in lots of light and a commanding view of the channel. I was all ready to buy it, but was informed that it was the Governor's Mansion and was not for sale. The entire town knew of our arrival and everyone knew we were looking for a house. It was no surprise when I met a lady in the grocery store who said her family was leaving Juneau and would we like to see her house? Since they had five children we thought it might do, so we followed her home.

She lived on Starr Hill, almost at the top of the stairs that served as sidewalks, in a house that was larger than any we had yet seen. There was a playground right across the street and upstairs in the house were five little rooms, which could be called bedrooms, and were. But as the Huderts weren't quite ready to move, would we consider moving in with them for a few days until we could all get sorted out? We would and did.

It was a bit confusing at first, sharing the icebox and the stove and the washing machine, but we managed. Mike, Pete and Jon stayed in the bus for a few days and Jim and Dave stayed on with the Stokes so we weren't too crowded. But everyone had to eat and mealtimes were wild until Mrs. Hudert and I decided to share the cooking and feed everyone at once. It was wild then too, but a sort of controlled wildness. Between us there were fourteen children who seemed to appear at mealtimes, eat prodigious amounts of food, drink about ten gallons of milk, and then vanish.

As I put our leftover supplies away in the kitchen cupboards, it occurred to me that I didn't have to keep the rest of the peanut butter in the bucket. By then there was about a two-inch layer in the bottom of the sixteen-pound pail, so I started to dig it out. There appeared to be a lump in the middle of this layer. Thinking it merely a lump of peanut butter, I put the spoon under it and lifted it out. To my horror I discovered the lump was a dead mouse. The entire thing went into the garbage then: pail, peanut butter and mouse. I wondered how long it had been there and decided I would tell no one.

I couldn't believe my eyes when I saw children playing outside at 10:00 p.m. They were in the playground shooting baskets and swinging on the swings, racing around and yelling and it was the middle of the night! My children would never be allowed to… hmm, did I just see Sally Ann out there, too? I thought she'd gone to bed. Well!

Starr Hill was a perfect choice for us; the hospital was two blocks away down the hill and the elementary school was four blocks down the same street. High School was farther away and the boys would have to walk, but I am a firm believer in having children walk to school. They have all that energy and might as well use some of it by getting the exercise and fresh air of the walk. An elderly, retired teacher once told me that children deserve the privilege and privacy of the walk to school.

There seem to be all those clubs here that men like, where they clasp hands and whisper things to each other. Women's clubs, too, even one called the Stitch and Bitch Club, which I hope I can join. Churches and bars are everywhere, as are gift shops. Also lots of rummage sales and even, so help me, Cub Scouts!

The town itself is dirty with mud, for even the paved streets have rivulets of mud trickling down them from the mountains above, and also with dog-doo. Apparently all the dogs in town use the sidewalks; I guess they have to, as the yards are so tiny. The stores are quaint but so is everything here. I love it all — except the dog messes. Some roads do lead out of town but stop about fifteen or so miles to the north and ten to the south. They stop at the edge of the wilderness. The street our house is on ends at the top, where it turns into a trail leading to the top of the mountain.

All kinds of wild game abound here: deer, bear, moose, ducks, geese, grouse, salmon, crab and clams — all to be had for the hunting or gathering. Berries of all kinds grow profusely everywhere. There are blueberries, red and blue huckleberries, salmonberries, low- and high-bush cranberries, strawberries and crowberries. All you need is a bucket with a bell on it, to scare the bears.

But my goodness, what a crazy place to build a town! There is hardly any flat ground at all; the stairs start almost at beach level and continue on up the hill until it becomes too steep to build at all. The stairs are wood and some of the side streets, like the one we live on, are dirt. Which means mud mostly. Some of the older stores are built on pilings and the odd, extremely high tide still comes up underneath them. At low tide you can smell the mud flats inside the stores. Juneau was built here, starting out with a few tents, because the gold was here, only a mile or so up the creek.

There is an abandoned house directly uphill from us. It is all boarded up and spooky. Neighborhood gossip has it that there is an open well inside, so children are told never, never to try to go in. But, of course, they all try it at least once. And I know there is no open well or anything else dangerous there because I too looked through the crack in the boards over the window. Nothing but dank gloom.

One plus about living on Starr Hill is that nearly every mother on the hill can look right down into the Chicken Yard and see if her kids are behaving. If not, up goes the window and she leans out to yell, "You get in here right now!" No psychology here, just good old-fashioned threats. The Chicken Yard? That's what they call the playground across the street from our house. It is the only level spot on the hill, having been dug out many years ago as a place for the nuns who run the hospital to keep chickens. They liked to have fresh eggs for their breakfasts and for the patients in the hospital.

Jack can and does walk to both the hospital and the office but we will get a car soon so we can take rides out the road to visit friends or just to carry home the groceries. One grocery store does make home deliveries so that is the one I patronize. There is one clothing store and I must say it is kind of fun to have almost NO choice at all or at best a choice between two dresses only. Makes life simple. In the old days, I'm told, when the red lights shone down on South Franklin Street, stores had elegant, costly gowns, and many of them full of lace set in satins of brilliant colors. So it must have been much more fun to go shopping, but no decent woman would have been caught dead wearing one of those gowns, no matter how much lace it had. And no woman would be caught dead in the doctor's office on Wednesday afternoons either, for that was the day the ladies of the night had their physical exams. But prostitution was outlawed two years ago when Alaska became a state so the glamour has gone, leaving just the tiny houses, which are now gift shops and boutiques, and clothing stores with two choices.

My new friend and neighbor, who had told me all this and who had grown up in Juneau, said when she was a young child it used to be a special pleasure for her when her father, holding her by the hand, had to go past these little houses, for they all had names that fascinated her. There was Daisy, and Feathers, and Bubbles and Flower. These names were painted on little board signs, which hung over the doorways. She really had loved those names and dearly wanted to change hers from Mary Lou to something more exotic, like Rosina Rubylips or Heavenly Hanna.

She told me other stories, too, but the one I like best is the one she told me about the miners.

The gold mine was built, as was everything else, on the side of the mountain and there was a trail leading from the mine to the homes of the miners, which were on the same street as our house. The men used to walk to and from work every day. At night, she said, you could see a long line of little twinkling lights moving slowly down the mountain as the miners, wearing headlamps, wound their way slowly homeward. And again in the morning the same long line of little lights would be seen traveling up the mountain as they all went to work again. What a pretty sight it must have been.

"And," she said, "every store in town was open twenty-four hours a day because the mine was open too, and you could go downtown at any hour and buy whatever it was you wanted." How convenient! Should you find yourself at 1:00 a.m. suddenly needing a pair of earrings or a dog collar or even a two-pound T-bone steak, all you had to do was go get it.

Epilogue

November, 2001

Jack remembers:

In my memory, our bus trip to Alaska is of a pleasant adventure interspersed by a few occurrences that were less than happy. The main one of these was the breakdown in Manitoba when the engine seized up because of the unnoticed loss of oil due to a broken oil tube. My chief worry had been that a non-repairable catastrophe would happen to the bus, necessitating aborting the trip and returning to Falmouth, an eventuality that would have been not only discouraging, but also expensive and embarrassing. The good fortune that this breakdown happened in a location where sophisticated repair services were immediately available was astonishing and reassuring; thereafter I worried less about the bus. In fact, the same oil line broke again north of Fairbanks but the falling oil pressure was noticed before harm was done. After that we switched to a flexible, vibration-proof hose. The hot, humid, mosquito-plagued night that preceded this breakdown stands out in memory as well.

Another highlight was the excitement of driving the Yellowhead Route in a vehicle that was just inches narrower than the roadbed with a sheer rock wall on one side and an equally sheer precipice on the other. The fact that large logging trucks were using the road was somewhat encouraging, but also instilled the fear that we might meet one and be forced to back up over the same road that was terrifying in forward gear. Having been inured, in later years, by similar or worse roads in Baja California, the Yellowhead Route doesn't seem so bad in retrospect but we hadn't had that experience yet.

The most frightening occasion for me was when David and I overturned in our canoe, early in the trip, due to our inexperience in fast water and the fact that we had been assured there would be none in this river. It really wasn't dangerous and would have been worth only a good laugh if I had been alone or with another adult. But with David it was another matter altogether.

The single most memorable location was certainly Atlin, B.C., where we spent an enjoyable week panning for gold; watching miners using large high-pressure water hoses to "sluice" ore from a hillside; gathering wild watercress; fishing in Lake Atlin and generally enjoying the beauty and tranquility of the place.

Nearing the end of the trip, I can recall feeling pangs of disappointment when we were running out of places to investigate and still had not found a satisfying spot to settle. Must we return to Falmouth? Our discovery, or rediscovery, of Southeast Alaska settled those pangs, and I think we made the right decision.

Sally remembers:

Last week as I rummaged through a drawer full of odd little bits and pieces of my life, my fingers found the small, black stone with the white X on it — the one I had picked up at Toad River. As I rolled it around in my hand I thought again of that sunny day on the highway where a picnic lunch by a very old log cabin had changed the course of our lives.

Jack saved as many of the cigar boxes as he could get his hands on and to this day they sit in his workshop, full of handy items like nuts and bolts and washers. A little serendipity here: Last night I was at Tom's house for dinner. This is a weekly occurrence because Jack plays bridge with a group of fellow devotees and I hate bridge, so I go to Tom's and we have dinner together. This night I asked him for a pencil. He reached across the table, pulled a cigar box from under some papers and rummaged around in it.

"Where did you get that?" I asked him.

"Oh," he replied, "I've had it as long as I can remember."

At least one duffel bag still exists, one of those that Jack sewed back in Falmouth. We use it when we go to our cabin in the real wilderness, a mere mile away, on Pleasant Island. We have our cake and eat it too in this way: We live here in solid comfort with all sorts of labor-saving devices but, when the mood strikes us to have a little wilderness living, off we go for a week or so. It is restful there, without the telephone or fax or "machines at meal-time." Just the cathedral of trees with its thick carpet of moss and the occasional deer or otter for company at twilight. Then, it is back home for hot showers, clean clothes and white sheets. Now that I think of it, that zipper that leaked rainwater onto my face so frequently never did get fixed until we got to Juneau. Then we rolled up the tent and stored it away for twenty years before we used it again.

In the last ten years or so, moose have moved into our part of the world, giving us an abundant supply of meat, which is so good it makes store-bought beef insipid. In all the years we've been here never once have I been served roast moose nose, and I'll be sure to let the world know if I ever see a wilted salad. You never know. As for stew thickeners, flour is a great substitute for rabbit droppings, especially since no rabbits live here. Do you recall mention of the large white house in Juneau, which I had hoped to be able to buy but couldn't because it was the Governor's Mansion? I did get to live there; not as governor or even as governor's wife, but as cook. I loved the house and the job but, as we had moved away from Juneau by that time, travel back and forth by air was difficult and expensive. So I left the range at the mansion, an electric one, for mine at home, which used wood. But all that is another story so I shall stop here and say that we are happy to have made the move — and yes, we have been to France several times but always look forward to coming home to the serenity and the friendly faces of Alaska.